EXPAND YOUR BUBBLE

EXPAND YOUR BUBBLE

AMY CARST

For information, visit www.amycarst.com

Library of Congress Cataloging-in-Publication Data

Names: Carst, Amy: author

Title: Expand Your Bubble

Description: United States: *evolution of id*

Library of Congress Control Number: 2018904196

ISBN 9780692102749

Cover by ATMODESIGN

CONTENTS

DEDICATIONS vii

ix

1. PROLOGUE 1

2. THE UNEXPECTED SOCIAL EXPERIMENT
5

3. EMBRACE THE BLACK SHEEP WITHIN 15

4. DON'T BE AFRAID OF THE BOOGEYMAN
17

5. THE STORY OF MALAYAKA HOUSE 23

6. FINDING MY TRIBE 29

7. STRUGGLE 37

8. ROBERT 41

9. PERFECTION, PROGRESS AND POWER
45

10. THE DEEPER MEANING OF REBELLION
49

11. PIZZA NIGHTS 57

12. THE INTERVIEWS 59

13. SQUATTING 61

14. THE GIFT OF ANGER 71

15. THE AFRICAN 81

16. THE COMMUNIST 95

17. TRANS 105

18. FROM THE DRAGON MOM OF JACK 133

19. THE VISIONARY 143

20. RESIST 151

21. THE REFUGEE 155

22. THE PASTOR 165

23. THE GILDED CAGE 179

24. LONGEVITY 191

25. THE ADDICT 199

26. THE ARAB WORLD 207

27. THE BUDDHIST 219

28. THE MEDIUM 225

29. POETIC JUSTICE 235

30. STREET KIDS 243

31. BE YOUR OWN ARCHITECT 247

32. ACKNOWLEDGMENTS 259

DEDICATIONS

Julie, you were the first person to tell me I wasn't crazy. You validated the seeker within, when I needed it most. I'd call you my best friend, but you are family to me.

Robert, this book wouldn't exist if our paths hadn't crossed. I will never be able to thank you enough for all you have given me without even knowing it. My life changed the day we met. You are my mentor but, more importantly, you are my friend.

A few years ago, I was fortunate to meet Professor Noam Chomsky—linguist, philosopher, activist, and the author of over one hundred books. Since then, I have reached out to him on numerous occasions to ask his opinion about one thing or another I was working on. He has always returned a thoughtful response.

When I began writing this book, I asked Professor Chomsky if he would consider contributing something, however small; it just wouldn't be complete without his voice. He said he was pleased that I was able to carry on with this most important work and offered me the quote below. Receiving this gift, from one of the most influential and important minds of our time, will remain one of the highlights of my life for the rest of my days.

It is easy to look at what is happening in the world and to succumb to despair. The right way—the way you have taken—is to grasp the opportunities that always exist and to carry forward the unending struggle to achieve a better world. ~ Noam Chomsky

I grew up in a typical white, middle-class American family. My parents divorced when I was five; they remained amicable, at least in front of my brother and me. I went to a public school in a "good area," played sports, got a part-time job at the local diner, and hung out with other kids who looked like me, thought like me, and whose parents looked and thought like my parents.

Pretty basic stuff.

I started getting into trouble during my high school years, but I won't talk about that; none of it was very book-worthy at that stage. I moved out the day I graduated, which also happened to be my eighteenth birthday. The way I saw it, there were two options: go to college or be a loser. My grades were awful, and I had hated every second of high school, so college wasn't on the horizon for me. By the rules vested in the process of elimination, I was a loser.

Self-identifying as a loser is not without its

privileges. When we lower our standards to such an extent, our individual choices become less significant. What does the outcome matter when you've given in to being a loser? For years, I made an unconscious decision to do absolutely nothing with my life.

By the age of twenty, I was married to a man who was ten years my senior. He was a good guy, but we had nothing in common, and if I recall correctly (because this part of my life is a blur) I only got married because it felt like I was actually doing *something*. We basically fought for four years. And then, finally, it was just over. One night, I stayed out partying until the early morning hours and came home to an unhappy husband. We screamed at each other for about five minutes; I told him I didn't want to be married anymore and stormed out for the last time. Two months later, I found out I was pregnant with the child of the bartender at our local Olive Garden.

OK, before you start judging me, let's fast forward to today. Mr. Olive Garden bartender (whose real name is Jesse) is my husband of fifteen years and is father to my three children, and we are quite in love thank you very much. Who'd have guessed that outcome?

But the road to bliss is often paved with a lot of

shit, and we certainly trudged through our fair share. We've been through bankruptcy, foreclosure, and some minor marital transgressions. For the first ten years of our marriage, we dealt with all of the above, in addition to raising three kids and not really liking ourselves. It was certainly not the recipe for a healthy relationship, or life for that matter.

I'm thirty-nine years old, and I love my life today. How did that happen? I can tell you; it wasn't true love and hard work that saved us. I didn't forego my loser identity due to maturity and the responsibility of raising three children. It was an uphill battle, and neither my husband nor I have emerged unscathed. But scars can be beautiful, and each of mine is the equivalent to a year at an Ivy League school. Without my scars, both figurative and literal, I would still be my insecure, confused, destructive former self. The thrill-seeker in me is still very much alive, but I've learned to satisfy the seeker with more fulfilling thrills.

But I digress.

My story wouldn't amount to anything worth telling without the rich cast of characters that have helped shape me into the person I am today. When I say "the person I am today," this is not to say that I am now an enlightened or superior creature. No, I am just as dysfunctional and messy as ever. I still have a tic disorder, get too easily stressed when it comes to my kids and husband, am a poster child for disorganization, drink more than I would like to (I'm working on that) and will never, ever be good with money. But I love my life now—despite the hurdles—and that's the crucial difference.

***

Expand Your Bubble is a collection of interviews with people from diverse backgrounds, cultures, races, and lifestyles. Each person interviewed has opened my eyes to something profound, and my life is richer for it. After sharing some of my personal journey, I'll introduce you to Africans, Communists, refugees, the ultrawealthy, squatters, activists, mothers, addicts, Christians, Buddhists, best-selling authors, entrepreneurs, and more.

The Malayaka House orphanage in Entebbe, Uganda has played a significant role in my journey. For this reason, I am donating all profits from the sale of this book to Malayaka House.

Enjoy!

THE
UNEXPECTED
SOCIAL
EXPERIMENT

I use Airbnb to rent an apartment attached to my house. It's been lucrative, sometimes fun, and often stressful, but the process has also provided something unexpected. My husband has always enjoyed people-watching. He can sit somewhere for hours and watch random people walk by, quietly observing each passing stranger, most of whom disappear from eyesight and memory within seconds. People-watching has never really been my thing, at least not in the traditional sense. Maybe it's the randomness of it all; a never-ending sea of unknowns walking by can be visually engaging, but we can't decipher much from these split-second observations. That's perfectly fine with my husband, though. He doesn't want to learn from passersby. For him it's meditative, relaxing, something to pass the time. I've never been very good at relaxing or passing the time.

So, when we started doing Airbnb, I was shocked to learn how much I actually *do* enjoy observing people. Before I scare anyone who may have stayed with us, let me be clear: I'm not observing anyone in the visual sense. Rather, it's a general feeling I get based on our email communication prior to the stay, our initial meeting upon arrival, any communication or lack thereof throughout the stay, and the guests' "style of departure."

We live in rural Vermont, close to a popular ski town with multiple craft breweries, art galleries, and organic farms. As such, most of our guests are middle-class, white American families coming to Vermont to take a break from city life and stressful corporate jobs. But we do get the occasional non-white person, foreigner, Muslim, or self-proclaimed redneck.

At the risk of making an offensive generalization, here are my observations. The middle-class, white American families have been generally wonderful at pre-arrival communication. Most are skilled at written communication and use the opportunity to paint a picture of who they are, explaining everything from the nature of their stay in Vermont to their daughter's PhD program at Harvard. Upon arrival, they are friendly but brief.

From that moment forward, it is as if they don't exist; curtains remain drawn (not that I'm peering into anyone's windows, mind you), the deck and grill sit untouched, and nobody emerges from the safety of their interior space, except to get in their SUVs and head to dinner.

Finally, their stay is marked complete by the absence of cars in the parking area and the receipt of an almost-boilerplate parting text, "Thank you for the lovely accommodations. Wish we could have shared a beer or glass of wine. Maybe next time!"

I'm not complaining. Some people are not particularly social, or they just want their privacy. Others might be very social but have such jam-packed itineraries that there's simply no time to have a beer with their Airbnb hosts. Hell, I've stayed in many an Airbnb and haven't always engaged with the hosts. But my little social experiment has been nothing short of fascinating. Exactly zero of the middle-class, white American guests have strayed from the scenario I laid out above. And exactly the opposite can be said for every non-white, foreign, or "redneck" guest that has stayed with us. Obviously, there *will be* some exceptions. But as of yet, there have been none.

The non-white, non-American, and non-middle-class guests we've hosted have used the deck, visited us at least once during their stay, and knocked on our front door to say goodbye and thank us before leaving. Some have even fed us; the Iranian family inviting us over for kebab was my favorite.

But what does all of this mean? Does being white, middle-class, and American make people less friendly? I don't think so. But I do think this demographic—*my* demographic —is suffering from an acute and pervasive loss.

The best word to describe what we are missing is "community." "Tribe" is a close second. But alas, these words are thrown around by the liberal elite so often that they too have lost their meaning. In fact, I was going to entitle this book *Finding Your Tribe*, but became annoyed with the word's overuse before I was half finished. Even so, I've found no better words to use. We have lost a profoundly important aspect of the human experience.

This loss of community is nothing new. Fifty years ago, it was due to an increase in our desire for material wealth, and what we had to do to earn money to obtain the material possessions we desired. It was work, work, work—even at the expense of friendships, family, and blood pressure. Today, our even more rapidly vanishing sense of community is still due to the desire to make money and obtain material possessions and status, but it's also due to an increase in our desire for knowledge, and our perception of what we must do to achieve that knowledge.

In 2018, knowledge is currency. Status is no longer dictated by the amount of money in our bank account but by the amount of knowledge in our mind. Whereas material possessions are the outward symbol of monetary wealth, the company we keep and books we read are the outward symbols of our intellectual wealth. Those born into white, middle-class American families are shaped by this ideal from birth. If we eat organic food, read Chomsky, travel the world, watch Indie films with subtitles and are skilled communicators—both oral and written—we are middle class, despite what our bank accounts might say. We have trashed the antiquated class systems that are based on monetary wealth alone. On one hand, this is great news! Being broke no longer means I have to feel inferior. I am rich with knowledge.

But nothing comes without a price.

Humans have had an insatiable quest for power since the beginning of our existence on Earth. Whether that power comes in the form of kingdoms, fame, money or knowledge, we will do just about anything to get it. Fifty years ago, we proved we were superior to the Joneses with outward displays of wealth—a nicer house and nicer cars, for example. Today, we prove we are superior to the Joneses with a diverse cast of friends, an exciting travelogue, and social media posts of the vegan, kosher, local, organic, halal, free-range, gluten-free meal we prepared for dinner this evening.

We all know that material possessions—or lack thereof—can still define and divide us, *if* we let them. And we usually do. Trailer-park Tara isn't likely to take a freshly-baked pie to her new neighbor, McMansion Mary, nor the other way around. But what if trailer-park Tara only lives in the trailer because she is getting "back to the land," teaching her children about the dangers of capitalism and using her affordable plot of earth to create an organic community garden to feed the less fortunate in her area? Can you say game changer? With knowledge being the new currency, Trailer-Park Tara is immediately elevated to middle class. Maybe Mary *will* make that pie now. And she'll probably tell her friends about her eccentric, funky new friend—just like when she shared the story of her new black friend, Lakshme Moon (a.k.a. yoga instructor), and the time Lakshme came over to discuss race relations in America (a.k.a. teach yoga).

So, what's the problem? Finally, we have been able to transcend the shackles of wealth-based class systems. But in doing so, flesh and blood human beings have taken a backseat to the stories we tell. A social media post doesn't have to accurately represent your life, only the life you want to convey. And it's no different in real life; we can be anyone we want to be, and that comes with an immense amount of pressure. It's hard work coming off as smart, cultured, strong, witty, beautiful, compassionate, and creative. But dammit, we try.

We may preach the liberal value that differences are good, and should be both tolerated *and* respected. But the reality is, we are not accepting of differences unless they are of the coveted variety. For example, fifty years ago, very few white American, middle-class people would have had a mixture of gay, black, and Muslim friends. Today, it's actually cool to have a gay friend, black friend, or Muslim friend. Hell, you can even throw in a transgender friend for good measure—but not a redneck friend. That's still not cool. Who knows, in a few years, Billy Bob and his brother Cletus might be the trendiest arm candy at the Sundance Film Festival, but for now, they'll just damage your rep.

All that being said, it should be fairly obvious where I'm headed with this book. Acceptance should not be exclusive to groups who are currently...*ahem*...accepted. If you are only accepting of socially-accepted people, you are not practicing acceptance. That's a mouthful, and rightfully so; it says a lot.

In order to accept others, however, we must first accept ourselves. When I was in my twenties and early thirties, amidst marital and financial troubles and a perceived lack of purpose in my life, I had not yet accepted myself. My problems were all-consuming and filled me with shame.

Like most humans, I lived in a bubble with other people who looked and thought like me, who had relatively similar upbringings and belief systems, and who were of the same socioeconomic status. As a result, I adopted the same ideas about my problems as they would have in a similar situation; the bankruptcy, job loss, and marital woes all seemed to be insurmountable problems that would plague me for the rest of my life.

But what if they weren't actually problems at all?

There *are* problems in this world—real ones. Poverty and stage four cancer are problems, for example. Child abuse is a problem. Climate change is a problem. But filing for bankruptcy because of overdue Lexus payments and credit card debt—the product of hundreds of dinners out, massages, and salon visits—is *not* a real problem. A bump in the road? Yes. A lesson in how to do it better next time? Definitely. But a problem? No.

There are very real problems in the world. Working toward eradicating them is the most effective way to put your perceived "problems" in perspective and start enjoying your life.

3

EMBRACE THE BLACK SHEEP WITHIN

One of the best ways to lead a fulfilling life is to utterly and totally ignore everything that society teaches you. Be a black sheep. That advice would have been really helpful for me about twenty years ago; I was always a black sheep but never embraced it. The other rebels I knew identified as punk or goth or "heads," but I still hung with the mainstream kids, the same friends I'd had since childhood. I didn't want to be a black sheep, I just was.

Being a black sheep can be powerful and liberating *if* you learn to embrace it. I stress the word *learn* because we are not raised to embrace our differences. Yes, parents might say things like "Don't follow the crowd," "Be your own person," or "Differences are good," but they don't actually practice what they preach, nor do they want their children to. Thus, it is quite rare indeed for a young person to embrace being a black sheep.

Even today, as my fortieth birthday nears, I am sad for the young me—not because I didn't fit into a mold but because I always *wanted* to. The goth kids and the punk kids were proud to be different (or at least that was my perception). I was ashamed. I was different, swimming in a sea of normal kids, while pretending to be normal. That's what makes me sad. I was an awesome kid but didn't know it. And that intense need to fit in would continue throughout my early adult years, into my thirties. The real me wanted to travel the world, live in a conversion van, make life a never-ending adventure. But my desire to assimilate was too powerful; the black sheep within remained in that suffocating white sheep costume for nearly two decades. (That's not a racial reference, by the way).

Looking back, I can't believe I lived that way for so long. I just needed to see another path. And when I did, there was no going back.

4

DON'T BE
AFRAID OF THE
BOOGEYMAN

During my teens and twenties, I hadn't yet learned that breaking rules can be an incredibly good thing. I was still breaking them the old-fashioned way, by acting out: skipping school, stealing my mom's car before I was old enough to drive, sneaking out at night, shoplifting, and doing some gateway drugs. Then I started doing some harder stuff, got married way too young, got divorced, got a DUI, and continued blindly walking in circles, always ending up exactly where I had started.

Nobody would have called me an anarchist or a dissident. More than one person probably called me a loser.

By my late twenties, I was tired of being a loser. I had traded the highs of partying for the highs of material success. I became an insurance broker and financial adviser, bought a Lexus and a house we couldn't afford, used my student loan refund checks to buy high-end furniture, racked up thousands in credit card debt, considered getting breast implants (but didn't have the money or enough available credit), got weekly massages, and exaggerated the amount of money I was making to impress the shit out of people.

I still wasn't happy.

So, a few years into this ridiculous charade, I found myself searching for something different again. It was exhausting—this endless searching and never finding. My life was always so chaotic, fast-paced, and filled with one distraction after another. I needed clarity and focus. Time alone with my thoughts.

Through an online search, I found a Buddhist center up the road from my house in Harrisburg, Pennsylvania. Soon I was a regular fixture at the Blue Mountain Lotus Society's weekly sangha meeting. Every Wednesday night, Sensei Tony, the charismatic Buddhist minister who ran the center, held a Dharma talk. This weekly meeting became like church for me, an atheist who had always longed for some semblance of ritual in my life. It was also very grounding. I loved the chanting, the ritual, and walking up to the altar to light the incense.

For the first time ever, I had found a space to sit alone with my thoughts, to actually contemplate what I wanted out of life.

I was unhappy. My kids and husband were the only things that mattered, yet I was generally too stressed and distracted by financial obligations to really appreciate them. During one of Sensei Tony's Dharma talks he said, "Look around at your possessions and ask yourself—about each one—do I have this because it truly makes me happy, or because of how other people will perceive me?" That was a lightbulb moment for me; *everything* I owned was for the sole purpose of impressing other people. All of my financial stress was rooted in material possessions that I didn't even want. For years, my sense of self-worth had been directly linked to material possessions.

It didn't take long for me to act on this new discovery.

Within a few months, we had walked away from all of our debt. The car loans, the credit cards, the mortgage. I'm not saying I'm proud of it, but I'm not saying I'm ashamed either. It would have taken us a decade to get out from under all of that shit.

With three young children at home, I couldn't stand the thought of prolonging the stress another day. We had to start with a clean slate—learn from our mistakes and move forward with wisdom and clarity.

But reinventing yourself isn't easy when you're surrounded by people who have known you for a lifetime. How could I be a successful insurance broker with a Lexus one day, and a hippy with a beat-up conversion van the next? The truth is, I could have done *exactly* that. Friends and family may have initially been confused, but my new narrative would have been as easily accepted as the old one...eventually. At the time, however, I didn't know any better. In my mind, moving to a new place and starting over was the only option. And I'm glad we did. You don't need to get out of Dodge to reinvent yourself, but in our case, moving from Pennsylvania to Vermont was one of the best decisions we ever made.

Before we hit rock bottom, walked away from our worldly possessions, and moved to Vermont, fear was holding me back from becoming everything I could be. Pregnant with my third child at thirty, I'd lie in bed each morning, paralyzed by an overwhelming sense of dread about financial problems. This fear was preventing me from moving forward, from realizing the limitless solutions to what I perceived as insurmountable problems. The Amy I presented to the world was a strong, confident, independent woman. Meanwhile, the real me was riddled with insecurities. I was terrified of failing in front of everyone who judged me. But all of it—from the DUI to the bankruptcy—paved the way for my life today. By surviving failure after failure and personal disaster after personal disaster, I was accidentally learning that society's "problems" are like the boogeyman; they can scare the shit out of you, but they can't actually harm you. Well, except for the drunk driving part. *That* can harm you.

I began to realize that even my most shameful failures couldn't destroy me. The fear of being judged that I'd carried around for so long began to disappear. It was liberating.

I still had no idea what I wanted to do with my life, but I was beginning to learn what I didn't want, and that can be just as powerful.

5

THE STORY OF MALAYAKA HOUSE

Before continuing *my* story, I want to share the story of Malayaka House. This special place, as you will soon learn, is like a second home to my family. Indeed, this book would not exist without it.

***

In 2005, an American by the name of Robert Fleming was in Uganda when he noticed a very pregnant woman living in the street outside of his hotel. Being a kind and compassionate human being, Robert approached the woman to see if she needed help.

In addition to being homeless and near term in her pregnancy, she was mentally ill. The woman told

Robert her name was Sara. She was confused; in some moments, she had been a teacher. Other times, she had been a nurse. At no point during their conversations did Sara acknowledge she was pregnant.

Robert continued to visit Sara each day, hoping to find her when she went into labor. It was the rainy season, and he knew that the child would not survive if Sara gave birth alone in the middle of the night.

Which is exactly what *almost* happened.

Robert found Sara in labor late one night. He helped her into his truck and sped to the hospital in Kampala, Uganda's capital city. As soon as they arrived, Robert went to a nearby room to sleep. He awoke a few hours later—disturbed by an ominous silence—and immediately went looking for Sara and the baby.

He found Sara in a bathroom, covered in blood, splashing water all over herself and the bathroom. There was no baby.

Robert found the missing newborn—a girl—in a trash can, alive but suffocating from mucus in her mouth and nostrils. He grabbed the infant, umbilical cord still attached, swiped the fluids from her mouth, and rushed her to the nurses.

This is where the story gets crazy.

Once the baby was cleaned up, her umbilical cord removed, and her health confirmed, the doctor brought her back to Robert.

"The mother is refusing the baby. We have nowhere to take her. You brought her here; you must take her home."

Robert had never wanted children.

An hour later, he was driving back to his hotel in his pickup truck, with a newborn baby in his lap.

He went straight to the women working at the hotel's front desk. "How do I care for her? What do I feed her?"

The women explained that he would need to get diapers and formula. They told him how to care for this tiny, motherless human.

Robert called his own mother. He told her what was going on, that he would stay in Uganda until he found a safe place to take the baby. Then he would return home.

A few days later, the police knocked on Robert's hotel-room door. They had another child. Three-year-old Bobo was the size of a six-month-old infant, with a broken femur and burns all over his body. He didn't speak, didn't even make any noises. Robert thought the child would die. But Bobo survived. Then came Viola; she was about eleven years old and had an infected wound on her leg. She didn't speak either. Next, the police arrived with six-month-old triplets, sick with pneumonia and malaria.

Robert soon realized that *nobody* was coming to rescue these children. He had two choices—abandon them and return to his easy life teaching tennis and traveling the world, or remain in Uganda indefinitely.

That was thirteen years ago. Today, Malayaka House is home to nearly fifty children; Robert, Bea, the aunties (local women who care for the children); and a host of volunteers from around the world.

Malayaka House isn't just a halfway point for poor souls. It's a home, a family. The children don't get "adopted out." This is their tribe for life. They become brothers and sisters.

And, living in a country with over eighty percent unemployment for people under the age of thirty, Robert knew his kids needed more than just traditional schooling. In addition to enrolling everyone in private school, Malayaka House has developed several in-house businesses to provide vocational training for the kids as they grow into adults. These businesses also employ the adult children and generate income for the orphanage, in an ongoing effort to one day be financially sustainable. Malayaka House runs a pizza restaurant and a mozzarella cheesemaking business, an I.T.

department, a permaculture farm system, a craft business, and a safari company.

Viola, the eleven-year-old girl from the story above, is now twenty-four and the first to go to University. She is studying to be a social worker. Bobo, that malnourished baby with broken bones and burns across his body, is now a joyful, energetic, 5'10" 16-year-old. I consider him my second son. And Malayaka—the girl who started it all—is a healthy, happy thirteen-year-old with a big, loving family and a future of limitless possibilities.

Robert's kindness and compassion toward one woman—thirteen years ago—has resulted in an entire community of healthy, joyful children with bright futures, and confident, financially independent adults who are creating positive change in Uganda.

And it's been good for him too.

6

FINDING MY TRIBE

Moving to Vermont brought about immediate positive change, but the road remained quite rocky for several years. I still felt lost.

After I'd worked for a year and a half in marketing at a tennis resort, I was itching to do something else. My brain wouldn't shut off; one minute I wanted to go live with Inuit tribes in northern Quebec and document their lives, the next I wanted to sell everything and homeschool the kids while traveling throughout North America in an RV.

Somewhere along the line, my scattered ideas came together in the form of a children's tea company, the Groove Tea Project (so called because each tea was named after a song). Cathy Stevens-Pratt, a local woman and one of the most talented artists I've ever met, did the funky, whimsical artwork for the tea tins. The Groove Tea Project was guaranteed to be a success!

But it wasn't.

Fortunately, by this point in my life, I was starting to see each failure as a mini-success, and the tea was no exception. When I was selling tea at shows, I also brought some coffee along for the non-tea drinkers. It wasn't long before I realized that *everyone* wanted coffee.

The decision to focus solely on coffee was an obvious one, but deciding to turn the business into a charitable venture held more significance than I could have possibly known at the time.

The plan was to import the coffee from Chiapas, Mexico and donate a portion of the profits to an orphanage in the same area. I started communicating with coffee farms in Chiapas, receiving shipments of coffee samples from throughout the region, and planning a visit to the farms.

Finally, I felt that high coming back to me—the one I used to get from skipping school, or doing a line of cocaine, or buying a Lexus. But this time, the high didn't immediately crash to a low. It lingered, even grew. For the first time, I knew what it meant to feel fulfilled.

While I was supposed to be marketing tennis

packages, I was researching coffee and working on a business plan. This new project filled my days and nights. It was exhilarating. My husband and I would sit up late at night talking about how to market the coffee, where to sell it, what kind of online presence we needed, and how we would work with the orphanage in Chiapas. But it was still very early in the game. We hadn't even decided which orphanage home or homes to work with.

I was at my desk "working" one day when Josh, a friend and co-worker, came into my office. He told me that Robert Fleming, a tennis instructor who had started an orphanage in Uganda, was at our club for the summer, teaching tennis because fundraising for the orphanage hadn't been successful that year. Tennis was the best way he knew of to make some quick money. Josh had told Robert about my coffee idea and he wanted to meet me and hear more about it.

Robert Fleming wanted to meet *me??!!*

I still remember the day I met him as clearly as if it were this morning. I told him about the coffee project, moving to Vermont, how I'd always wanted to travel. Robert listened intently and asked lots of questions. Then he said something that would change my life.

Robert: *You should come to Africa, to Uganda.*

Me: *I would love to go to Uganda! But how would I do that?*

Robert: (pause) *It's easy, you just get on a plane and come to Uganda.*

Three months later, I was on a plane bound for Uganda with my ten-year-old daughter.

***

The day I met Robert, I went home and shared the good news with my husband, Jesse. I was going to Uganda! Except he didn't see it as good news. In fact, he was adamant that I *not* go. For starters, nobody we knew had ever been to Africa…and wasn't Africa dangerous?

Then I made the mistake of showing Jesse the Malayaka House documentary, *Accidental Home*. Did I mention that Robert is good looking? Five minutes into the documentary, Jesse was like, "You're going to Africa with *that* guy?"

This was not going to be easy.

The next bump in the road involved the decision to take my oldest child with me. Thinking this would be the only time I'd ever get to Africa, I thought she should benefit from the experience as well. Now I wasn't just risking *my* life, I was also putting my daughter's life in danger. Everyone chimed in. Jesse was constantly bombarded with emails about the perils lurking around every corner in Africa.

This wasn't helping my case.

There was also the ever-so-slightly-inconvenient fact that I didn't have the funds to buy two tickets to Uganda. My mom agreed that this would be an experience of a lifetime for my daughter, so she offered to buy Ashlyn's ticket. In fact, she gave me her credit card number to purchase both tickets and said I could pay her back for mine.

So, there I was, a credit card number scribbled on the left margin of my notebook and two round trip flights to Uganda pulled up on the screen of my computer. Jesse—who was still vehemently opposed to the trip—was working evenings at that time, and the kids were all in bed. The only things between me and my destiny were a few keystrokes and some mouse clicks. My heart was pounding. I wanted nothing more than to buy those tickets. But I knew that Jesse would be furious. I also knew that I could never live with myself, or with him, if I didn't take this chance.

I bought the tickets.

The next morning, I told Jesse. He was pissed—no surprise there. But I think deep in his heart of hearts he knew that I *had* to go on this trip. For the next few weeks, as I prepared to leave, he was distant, but he wasn't awful. In fact, I secretly overheard him defending my choice to someone on the phone one day.

My mother and father were extremely supportive from the get go, which is fortunate, because I don't know if I would have followed through with my plan otherwise. Leading up to the trip, I received countless warnings from well-meaning people who worried for our safety. Even as I attributed their concerns to ignorance and "the West's misguided attitude toward the entire continent of Africa," I was privately beginning to wonder if they might be right. I had nightmares about giant spiders encasing us in gauzelike webs (think *Indiana Jones, Raiders of the Lost Ark*) and armed bandits ripping Ashlyn from my arms as I screamed, unable to save her due to the quicksand under my feet and the fierce, snarling lions surrounding me.

Of course, none of that happened.

While in Uganda, you are more likely to sip lattes in a coffee shop, see a feature film in 3D, or take a yoga class than see a lion, or even a spider...unless you're on safari. Then, if you're lucky, you'll see both.

I returned from Uganda a changed person but not because I had experienced an underprivileged culture that made me better able to appreciate my own. I was changed because of whom I met there—people from all walks of life and all corners of the world: Uganda, Albania, Spain, Germany, South Africa, Holland, Israel, Poland, and Mexico. These were interesting, fascinating people—people who were doing good. They were people who had exchanged material possessions for passion, traded stability for adventure. They were the weird outliers, the rebels, the wild ones. I had stumbled upon an entire flock of black sheep.

I had found my tribe.

7

STRUGGLE

Successful people frequently stress the importance of finding a mentor; the day we met, I knew Robert Fleming would be my mentor. His life—his entire being—exudes meaning and purpose, and humility. But there was more to it than that; there was a familiarity I couldn't quite put my finger on at the time. Robert knew he wanted something different from a young age—just as I did—but his journey began with ashrams in India, helping the sick and dying in Mother Teresa's homes in Calcutta, three-month-long silent meditations, and working with refugees in East Africa.

After meeting Robert and finding my tribe, I had a brief moment of feeling sorry for myself again. These people had been winning at life for years, even decades. All I could think about was how miserably I had wasted the first fifteen years of my adult life, flailing and floundering, desperately seeking something different but being too distracted and confused to find it.

Except I was wrong about these people. Some had been engaged in human rights work from an early age but most had landed here after years of "failing" at mainstream life. There were stories of relationships gone bad, financial difficulties, overcoming addictions or obesity, and even financially successful people who were just sick and tired of climbing the corporate ladder.

As time went by, I began to see the beauty of my own twisted, broken, messy path. If I had found myself in India at the age of eighteen, I may have never come back. Yes, I would have bypassed years of materialism and complacency, fear of judgment, and the pervasive feeling of being lost. But without all of those awful experiences, I certainly wouldn't be living the life I'm living today.

I know what it's like to have a fulfilling, exciting life, but I also know what it's like to be frustrated and lost. And I'm grateful for it. Had I found my path at eighteen, the juxtaposition of a life with purpose and a life *without* wouldn't be so apparent. I simply wouldn't appreciate my life the way I do today.

Further improving my sense of self-worth was the realization that *I* was actually inspiring the *others*.

The one thing we did not have in common, children, made my journey unique. Walking away from a "normal" life is hard enough. Doing it with three children, apparently, is an inspiration.

***

I acknowledge the great privilege inherent in my quest for purpose. My "struggle" during those years of dissatisfaction with my life, when I felt sorry for myself and wondered what stones I had to turn to find meaning and passion, was itself a luxury; I have never been worried about shelter, safety, or my next meal. I have never been denied a job or housing because of my race or ethnicity. I have never been terrified that my co-workers would discover my sexuality and torment or terminate me. I have never been assaulted or raped. I am healthy and able-bodied, and I gave birth to three healthy children who will never be harassed based on the color of their skin. My husband is a kind man. I'm the epitome of a privileged, white American woman.

My struggle was *always* internal.

8

ROBERT

There is this misconception about people doing humanitarian or social justice work: that they are saints who never mess up, who have exchanged freedom for helping others. But that is not at all the reality I have come to know. Instead, I see complicated, fascinating people who, rather than giving up freedom, have chosen a life of *total* freedom, and lots of hard work. Malayaka House's founder, Robert Fleming, is no exception.

Last year, when my family and I were in Uganda for a few months, I was having a cup of coffee and a cigarette with Robert on the porch of our rental house. He was telling me that when he found Sara in labor and took her to the hospital to deliver the baby, he had been wanting to do something meaningful with his life for a long time. He had spent years going back and forth to India and volunteering in Mother

Teresa's homes, always returning to Vermont to teach tennis in fancy clubs and live his easy life; he was beginning to feel like a charlatan.

Robert had been struggling with feelings of inadequacy when Sara—and consequently, Malayaka—came into his life. That motherless baby was just as much the answer to his problems as he was to hers.

We can all look back on some moment in our lives, the split second when something of significance began, or ended. A pivotal moment. The time when our lives changed, for better or for worse.

For me, that moment was the day I met Robert; I knew my life would soon change. Three months later, I was on a plane to Uganda with my young daughter. I didn't know why I was going to Uganda, nor what I would find there. But there was no question in my mind about whether or not to go. It was as if a previously unknown path had suddenly been illuminated. If I was a religious person, I would say that my prayers were answered that day. This book wouldn't exist if my path hadn't crossed with Robert's that summer afternoon, six years ago.

This book is essentially a collection of interviews with people who have helped shape my understanding of the world, and thus, my place within it. Ironically, the very individual who helped me the most, and who has achieved more in his life than anyone I've ever met, is the one who had the toughest time writing about his own experiences. Finally, I told Robert he was off the hook. I emailed him to say that I would share his story so that he could concentrate on doing what he does best, helping people with *real* problems. I did, however, ask him if I could share his email response below, in order to illustrate that even a man who has saved hundreds of lives can struggle with insecurity.

Thanks, Amy. I am happy to be off the hook. You do so much for me that when you ask me to do something I take it very seriously and try to do it in the best way I can...I hope you know this. For some reason I am afraid to say anything. On one hand, I am lacking confidence and self-esteem, and on the other hand, I am just worried that I'll write the wrong thing. Every time I try, I erase and criticize myself.

9

PERFECTION, PROGRESS AND POWER

It is easy to fall into the trap of thinking that our lives are a mess compared to the lives of those we look up to, those we wish to emulate. This is rarely the case, however. I once read a quote that went something like this: "We are always comparing our behind-the-scenes takes to everyone else's finished reel." Media and social media only make it worse.

All of our lives are messy, but we don't present the raw, unedited footage to the outside world. As a result, we live with the misconception that our problems are ours and ours alone. Nothing could be further from the truth; even people who appear to have their shit together have messy, complicated lives. In fact, those whose lives seem perfect may suffer most. Chaos is the natural order of things; attempting to conceal what comes naturally often leads to great distress. If nothing else, it's a lot of work!

Money doesn't solve problems, either. Studies have shown that once our basic needs— food, water, shelter and safety— are met, more money does *not* increase happiness. In fact, the opposite is often true. Many with fame and extreme wealth believe that their lives would be better if they didn't have so much. As a wise rapper once said, "Mo' money, mo' problems."

Yet, we always want more, and the grass is always greener. The desire for money, power, and perfection are manifestations of a deeply rooted, evolutionary characteristic unique to humans: progress.

Even as I write this book, I am thinking about what's next. I have wanted to be a writer since I was a young child. As I finish my first book—the culmination of just about every writer's career—I'm undervaluing this achievement. *My social media following isn't strong enough, therefore I'm not a real writer. I didn't get published by one of the big publishing houses, therefore I'm not a real writer.*

Progress, progress, progress.

The need for progress is innate to humans. It is why we have skyscrapers, the internet, lifesaving medicines, and the ability to fly. But it's also why we're never really satisfied. If ten years ago someone had told me that I'd be a professional writer by my mid-thirties and publishing my first book before my fortieth birthday, I would have been ecstatic. But as that reality plays out, I am too focused on the next milestone: getting published in the New York Times, thereby earning two dollars per word, or publishing a best-selling novel. *Then* I'll be a real writer.

Humans are always thinking of how happy we *will* be once the next goal is achieved. We think, *I'll be happy once I lose ten pounds; once I get the promotion; once I make six figures; once I buy my first house; once I buy a bigger house; once I get Botox; once I find love; once my daughter makes the baseball team; or once my son gets accepted at Harvard.* Since the advent of social media, the need for progress has accelerated. We can't scroll through Facebook or Instagram without seeing our "friends" reaching milestones we haven't yet reached, increasing the urgency to take that next step, and to take it soon.

You'll do a great deal for your mental health by reminding yourself daily that progress does *not* need to happen overnight. In fact, it's much more enjoyable when it doesn't. One of the benefits of having done a lot of drugs was learning that the greater the high, the harder the crash. Whether it's cocaine, a new car, or an acceptance letter from Harvard, the highs are better, and longer-lasting, when you take them slowly and space them out.

10

THE DEEPER
MEANING OF
REBELLION

Life is unpredictable, challenging, sometimes
frustrating, sometimes devastating. But it can also
be wonderful. I recently read an article about the
"new midlife crisis for women." It was one of the
most depressing articles I've read in a long time. It
described all of these American women in their late
thirties, forties, and early fifties (Gen X'ers) who
have everything they've ever wanted, except
happiness. They are stressed about money;
relationships; being the perfect mothers, wives and
friends; and paying for their kids' college
educations. I shared it with my best friend, Julie,
who replied back with, "Wow, that's dark." She's

right. Life is dark for many Americans, even though most of us wake up every morning bathed in light.

Full disclosure: I don't have money in savings. I don't have a retirement account. I am not saving to pay for my kids' college education. And I don't feel bad about any of it. If that's shocking to you, I'm not surprised. All of the above are cited as primary stressors for middle-aged, white, middle-class American women in the twenty-first century. I'm not entirely without a plan, however.

Consider college, for example. Most middle-class and upper-class Americans believe it is their duty to pay for their child's college education. When you venture out of this particular socioeconomic status and culture, however, that "obligation" all but disappears. If you have the money to pay for it, great. But if you don't, why throw your life away to give your kids something they may not even want, need, or appreciate?

My kids do well in school. If they want to go to college, they can work *their* butts off to get good grades and get scholarships. If their grades drop, they can try for athletic scholarships. If neither of those options work, they can apply for student aid and get student loans. If they don't want to acquire debt, they can go to Germany or any of the other countries that offer bachelor's degrees (with courses taught in

English) nearly free. And if that doesn't suit their needs, they can learn a trade. I mean, let's face it, unless your kid wants to be a doctor, lawyer, teacher, psychologist or work in some other profession that still requires a college education, college degrees are becoming less and less relevant in our rapidly evolving, high-tech world. *Who* you know, and how well you are able to adapt to change, are quickly becoming more important factors than a college degree.

As for my retirement, I make *decent* money as a writer and can work from anywhere in the world. If my future income isn't enough to live well in the U.S. when I'm seventy, I'll move to Ecuador, or Albania, or anywhere I can live well on a virtual, U.S. income. On top of that, I love writing and would be happy doing it until the day I die. This isn't a career from which I want to retire one day. This is my passion. I hope to be writing until I'm 90, 100, or 450, if the likes of Elon Musk and Yuval Noah Harari are right.

Find something you're passionate about, something you don't want to retire from. If you can't leave your current job right now, start your passion on the side. You don't need to make money from it now. If you love it, the money will come one day.

OK, so far so good, but what if I develop some

kind of disability that prevents me from writing well beyond my 300th birthday? Well, then I guess I'll collect disability from the U.S. government. And what if the U.S. government no longer pays disability? Well, that probably means the U.S. has gone to Hell—which is increasingly possible—and all the prepared planners are just as far up Shit's Creek as yours truly.

If the country goes to Hell, I still have my kids and loving husband. Certainly, *they* will take care of me. But what if I outlive my husband, and my kids don't want the burden? I mean, I didn't even pay for their college education!

For now, I'm holding out hope that one of the three will step up to care for their dear, ailing mom. We may not have paid for college, but we showed them the world and taught them to ask questions. They know that life can be whatever they want it to be. And if you ask me, that's worth a hell of a lot more than a bachelor's degree.

But what if I assume the worst—that the whole lot of 'em will turn their backs on me, even as I am too ill to write and the entire country has gone to Hell? Then what? Well, then it seems my life would be pretty awful anyway, whether I had a retirement savings or not.

I've chosen to enjoy the hell out of my short time

here, while doing what I can to make the world a better place. Lamenting about the past and worrying about the future is not only pointless, it impedes our ability to live the lives we want to live.

Society was created by flawed humans, and it continues to evolve based on the beliefs and ideals of flawed humans. Many of these flawed humans are in positions of power and they use that power, quite effectively, to control us. But we can choose to rebel. Rebelling isn't always easy, but it's intensely liberating.

Sometimes I rebel against something and then realize, *Oh shit, I should have followed the rules on that one.* But mistakes are part of life, whether we are following a path laid by others, or creating our own.

If your kids are getting into trouble today, hold on to the knowledge that rebellious teens often turn into passionate, adventurous adults. Teach them to question everything. Avoid sheltering them from the atrocities in the world. Pretending we live in a perfect, equal, peaceful society is downright cruel to our children. Sheltered children grow into adults who are unprepared to deal with the world around them.

Teach children tolerance, to love and to accept all humans. This is the best way to fight the world's atrocities—to raise the generation that will fight intolerance because they are aware, and because they have been taught to love. And tolerance will help them succeed. The world is increasingly small; for our children to be successful, they must learn to coexist with people of diverse backgrounds, races, religions, beliefs, cultures, abilities, and lifestyles.

I was talking to my eleven-year-old daughter the other day, explaining how fortunate she is to live in a time when she can love whoever she wants to love. I told her that even twenty years ago, when I was growing up, a white woman dating a black guy (or vice versa) was "taboo," and that it is still taboo in much of the country, and the world.

A person's soulmate could be of an entirely different race or religion, or live on another continent. Wouldn't it be sad if my daughter never found her soulmate because she thought she could only date white, middle-class American men?

Then I said to my daughter, "I just want you to know that if you come home one day with a partner named Billy Bob who is half-black, half-Asian, Muslim, transgender and in a wheelchair, we will love that person, as long as they are good to you." She looked at me and started tearing up, which made me start tearing up. Then she said, "Daddy would be crying, too." And I knew, at that moment, we are doing something right. For an eleven-year old child to tear up at the deeper meaning behind such a statement tells me that she gets it.

Love and acceptance is right. Anything else is wrong. Rebel against what is wrong. Teach your kids to do the same. And stop stressing about shit that doesn't matter.

11

PIZZA NIGHTS

For visitors, one of the best things about Malayaka House is Pizza Night. Every Tuesday and Thursday night, year-round, Malayaka House turns into a popular restaurant, opening its doors to Ugandans, NGO workers, pilots and flight attendants, soldiers in the American military, doctors, volunteers, and anyone else who wants to try the best pizza in Entebbe.

Pizza Night is an opportunity for people from all walks of life to connect and learn more about each other over a beer and slice of pizza. I've had some real breakthroughs at Pizza Night. Light bulb moments. Epiphanies. I've learned that most of my "problems" were not problems at all, and that my life can be whatever I want it to be. I know it sounds cliché: *you can be whatever you want to be.* We hear it all the time. But we rarely see it in action. When you see people, lots of people, who are actually living life on their own terms, it's incredibly empowering.

The different perspectives and diverse lifestyles I've encountered over the years, at Pizza Night and beyond, have shifted my thinking and given me the tools to create the life I want. I would not be where I am today without these people.

But I realize that not everyone can, or wants to, travel all the time. The reality is, those of us who live in the U.S. don't *need* to travel to benefit from the perspectives of others; this is still the most diverse country on Earth. Even so, getting out of our bubble is often easier said than done, and I was starting to feel guilty about keeping all this good stuff to myself. So, I decided to write this book, a collection of interviews with people who have given me the tools to create my best life.

As a writer, I could have told their stories. But then this book would have been just another white, middle-class American writer's perspective on the rest of the world. I thought they could tell their stories better.

And so, without further ado, here they are.

12

THE INTERVIEWS

Many of the interviews that follow are written in the person's own words. I have only edited for spelling, and in some cases, I've added, deleted or changed a few words for clarification. No content has been changed, and I've left most "stylistic" techniques, such as run-on sentences and CAPS, to allow the individual's unique voice to come through.

SQUATTING

Sometimes you meet somebody and immediately feel the urge to ask a million questions. You just sense their deep layers—of foreign experiences, different perspectives, and the knowledge of things you didn't even know existed. When I met Pim, I knew I wanted to know more about him.

Pim, a youthful, middle-aged Dutch man who lives in my town (a small Vermont hamlet of about 300 people) doesn't drive. This is fortunate for me because sometimes he needs to leave the middle of nowhere, and I am always happy for his company. Every month or so, we make the three-hour round trip to the "big city" of Burlington, and I get to ask him any question that pops into my head.

Pim has lived, or traveled to, just about everywhere. His stories are rich, inspiring, fascinating, and sometimes gritty. I found his experiences with the punk movement and squatting to be particularly interesting. Squatting was never something I understood or really thought much about, to be honest. In the past, if someone had asked me if I thought squatting was a positive thing or a negative thing, I'm guessing my gut reaction would have been to say negative.

I wouldn't say that now.

THE INTERVIEW
(Pim)

Squatting is the action of occupying an abandoned building or piece of land. It is a movement focused on resisting housing speculation, gentrification, and fighting the lack of access to affordable, decent accommodation. Every person has a fundamental human right to safe, habitable and affordable housing, and the right to live with security, peace, and dignity.

I was a kid when I first heard about squatting—watching footage on the news of evictions and riots in Amsterdam. Squatters would fight with the police, break open the streets, and throw bricks. Charges, burning cars, a burning tram. Tanks in the streets, mayhem, a disrespect for the old order. The squatters defended their buildings and their beliefs, their right to live life on their terms. I was a kid but felt an instant affinity: squatters stood for something, just like I should. I grew up in the Netherlands during the Cold War; I had trouble wrapping my head around the dumb world I was born into. I think I resented being here. I was instinctively weary of authority and its repressive structures. 'Ungrateful,' my parents said. 'Critical,' I believe. I questioned the middle-class sensibilities: money, status, the expectations of me, the neighbor's expectations of me. I needed to be in this world on my own terms and the hands-on, 'do it yourself,' contrary, engaged, autonomist mentality of both punk and the squatters movement suited me.

The first squat I moved into was a big and stately hotel, which had been empty for years and had seen much better days. It had its own grounds, a kitchen with twenty cookers (ovens), a restaurant, terraces, and many rooms, all en suite. The hotel was squatted by Bhagwan followers. They had travelled; some were foreigners: Israeli, American. All of them spent time in India. I found them interesting and exotic. We were the local kids; we came in to say hello, and I think the squatters found us entertaining too. We quickly decided that we would live there too. I don't think we even asked anybody.

The squat was completely disorganized. There

wasn't even a lock on the front door. Or running water, but everybody still used the toilets. When the toilets were 'full,' we used the bath tubs. Once the squalor got too much, we just moved into another room. Every drug addict in a fifty-mile radius moved in too. Skinheads showed up outside the building, intimidating us. The plans we had for the place [the Bhagwan people intended to open a restaurant and yoga studio] fizzled out then died. I think I felt overwhelmed: I wanted a slice of real life and real people, but this was more than I bargained for. I was seventeen and daunted by being on my own and having to take care of myself, and spooked by my surroundings, the lives of the addicts especially. But even though this squat was a missed opportunity, a lot of aspects of squatting appealed to me. The hotel was a forward-thinking place, inviting, full of possibilities, ideas, and plans. An experiment, socially, politically. An analytical and critical environment—resisting, angry, liberal, liberated. There was great equality and acceptance, unlike in any other place I had known outside of the hotel.

It wasn't very long before I moved into another squat. This time around, we organized ourselves much better and took care of the buildings we lived in. We were entrepreneurial, but not capitalists. We ran massive complexes containing housing, bars, clubs, theaters, performance spaces, cinemas, stores, record labels, radio stations, restaurants, galleries, artist work and rehearsal spaces, letterpresses, newspapers, and even a medical clinic. In every major city there was a 'squatters' consultancy'; aspiring squatters were informed on the legalities of squatting, and assisted with finding a building. A bag with all the tools necessary for opening a building could be borrowed. When a building was evicted, all of us would show up to barricade and defend the building. We fought back successfully, and we fought back for everybody. We weren't easily pushed over or pushed out. They knew we meant it.

We would pay 'rent' to the house and use this money to fix the building. One day a week was spent working on the squat, communally. Some of these places had stood empty for years; these buildings needed a lot of work and care. Often, we lived without electricity, heat, or running water. We were committed. It was never just a bargain.

It felt liberating not being weighed down by unjust, high, oppressive rents. Or by having your life imposed on or controlled by landlords and developers. It felt good not having those opportunistic scroungers in our lives: they don't belong there. The availability of affordable accommodation creates opportunity, possibility, risk-taking. The city of Amsterdam became more diverse, open, and thrived culturally because of the squatting: a healthier city. All residents benefitted from the discussion on how life in a city can be lived and organized, on how a city is run, issues of affordability and accessibility to housing. Who belongs in the city, and who does the city belong to? Culturally it was an interesting time too: everybody was welcome to whatever the squats coughed up: the bands, the art, the restaurants, the stores. We weren't sectarian, exclusive, or parochial.

It wasn't always perfect, but there was great freedom, respect, and tolerance in these squats: of class, color, background, sexuality, nationality, gender. We were a progressive, creative, hands-on and grassroots movement, critical of the world we lived in, and intent on making some adjustments. We were politicized and involved, outspoken. I think it is now clear that we asked the right questions and made some valid points on where our society seemed to be heading; just ask any teacher living the American Dream on a shoestring, while having to pay for their student's materials out of their own pockets. We defended our houses, freedoms, and beliefs. We had created a successful, working alternative to a money-driven, culturally impoverished, one-dimensional, and abusive system. Landlords, developers: they rarely add anything to society, but they often take from it. You have to see that for what it is: destructive, unjust, malignant; a simpleton, morally bankrupt approach to life.

Disputing existing structures, demanding fairness, and actually seeing your opinions connect with people doesn't make you popular with the authorities. So, when the city of Amsterdam clamped down on squatting, I was evicted countless times. We lost one building after the other. I remember coming home to find my house freshly bricked up, belongings inside. We also, somehow, lost the people's support. The media blamed us for violent evictions, and we started to get depicted as lazy, stoned, and destructive. I felt lost; I was nomadic and stayed on friend's sofas or slept in abandoned buildings. I was at University but found it hard to apply myself with so much disruption going on around me. I fell out of love with Amsterdam. The beautiful, lively, progressive culture we created was killed off. The city was becoming gentrified: boring, frumpy, over-organized. I left, travelled, and ended up in London, in a wild and happy international squat. We weren't part of a squatters' movement as such, or even a very political building; we hung out with other local squatters but mainly were a self-contained, content unit. That felt good: it gave me a space to lick my wounds and reconsider my place in the world.

I came to America. Accidentally, one of the first people I met in New York was a squatter friend from the Netherlands. She invited me to live with her in a just opened carcass of a building on the Lower East Side—a derelict place with most of the floors missing; no doors, stairs or roof; no water other than the water streaming down the walls when it was raining; no electricity, no heat. Our first winter was brutally cold. But the house was fixed up little by little [and was legalized eventually]. By then I had already left, annoyed and disillusioned. I felt I had little in common with most of the New York squatters. I was done squatting.

Now, years later, I dare to say that all of us former squatters still value living our lives independently, and on our own terms. They used to call us an 'alternative lifestyle,' but is it really? We were autonomous, adventurous, entrepreneurial, involved, political, community-oriented, accepting, unprejudiced, egalitarian, and free. How is that 'alternative'? We weren't capitalists, and so we refused to have our lives defined, dictated, or looted by capitalists.

It is upsetting to see that the cities I have lived

in [Amsterdam, London, Berlin, New York and Los Angeles] are rapidly being gentrified—becoming somewhat dull and exclusive places. Countless coffeeshops, but no bookstores, and impoverished in that sense. Many people I know: competent, educated, hardworking, are struggling to pay the rent, and to make ends meet. They are robbed of an even modest lifestyle. Adults sharing apartments, sharing the rent, and sleeping on the sofa. Or working two jobs and still scraping by. No time to take care of or spend time with their families and children. A growing underclass. Tens of thousands of people living in the streets or in their cars. Every interesting small store is closing down because they cannot afford the absurdly high rents. Then there's the 'trickle down landlordism': roommates taking advantage of roommates and screwing them for rent. Pompous buildings for the status conscious rising up everywhere, with pretentious names such as 'The Huxley,' 'The Residences,' 'Hollywood Versailles,' or 'The Phenix' [spelled just like that]. The regular city folks, the locals, are priced out. So are all the interesting people: the artists, the freaks.

Two years ago, I was living in a rent-controlled building in Los Angeles when I received a letter from my landlord, imposing an illegal rent increase upon us. They threatened repercussions to my credit should I dare to oppose their scam. According to the California Bureau of Real Estate, this was not in violation with their policies: I guess stealing and threatening people is perfectly ethical and within their guidelines. I ended up being thrown out of the building. It bothers me to see how little rights we have [left]. The other tenants were subjected to threats and abuses too. They were impossible to organize: worried about repercussions, intimidated, obedient. Tolerating being stolen from.

I see little fight in America, and that surprises me. I always thought of Americans as engaged, proud people. More and more, people in this country seem beaten, resigned to living a life of servitude under a sinister, oppressive system. These days, Americans earning a minimum wage cannot afford to rent a suitable place in any of the fifty states. Not that long ago, most families, with even a single breadwinner, could afford to buy a house. This is why we squatted; we knew this was coming. Just not this bad.

14

THE GIFT OF
ANGER

The ability to respond calmly when angry is the ultimate symbol of inner strength and confidence. It is power in its purest and most effective form. Over the years, I have mastered this ability in the outside world, but at home...not so much. These days, my kids and husband are the only people on Earth who ever see me lose my cool. I can calmly address someone who has accused me of encouraging "terrorists" to move to Vermont through my support of a controversial refugee resettlement, but when my nine-year-old leaves a clementine peel on my nightstand, I go insane.

In an effort to bring some peace to those who call me wife and mom, I read the book *The Gift of Anger: And Other Lessons from My Grandfather Mahatma*

Gandhi, by Arun Gandhi. In it, Arun tells of the two years he spent living with his grandfather on his ashram in India and how he has used his grandfather's teachings throughout his life. In addition to useful practices in the home, the book discusses ways to more effectively use our anger in work, politics, and social causes.

I see so much misdirected anger in the world today. Of course, there is neither more nor less today than at any time in history, but thanks to social media and the internet, it is more apparent, and thus, more dangerous. I fear this misdirected anger is the greatest threat to our ability to find common ground and move toward a globally equal society. This is especially an issue among men, who are taught at an early age to suppress emotions that are perceived as weak. As a result, many boys grow into men who struggle with how to manage anger, depression, and loneliness, and it often comes out in violent, aggressive, or—at the very least—ineffective ways.

In the *Gift of Anger*, Arun Gandhi explains that his grandfather experienced anger, like any human, but—through practice—learned to use his anger for good. Arun talks about our tendency to use anger as a way to dominate, to prove our truth to others. But the only person who must believe in your truth is you. Mahatma Gandhi said, "Truth stands, even if there be no public support. It is self-sustained."

Anger is useful, and necessary, in the fight for equality and peace, but misdirected anger puts us all at risk. I asked Arun if he had advice for parents—especially those of young boys—about how to raise adults with the capacity to use their anger for good and thus change the world. I also asked him how someone who is filled with anger after years of oppression based on race, religion, class, gender, or sexual orientation can use this anger as a tool?

Of course, such an answer cannot be found in a short interview nor in an entire book. But what *can* be found is what my friend Julie calls a breadcrumb. We are always looking for the definitive final answer to all of life's problems, when all we need is a single breadcrumb that will slowly but surely lead us in the right direction. The search for answers need not be a race. In fact, Mahatma Gandhi himself said, "Glory lies in the attempt to reach one's goal, and not in reaching it."

There are several useful breadcrumbs in my interview of Arun Gandhi. May they help you take one step in the right direction.

"If we are to teach real peace in this world, and if we are

to carry on a real war against war, we shall have to begin with the children." ~ Mahatma Gandhi

THE INTERVIEW
(Arun Gandhi)

Anger manifests itself in human beings for more reasons than just bad parenting. For centuries, we have been living in a society where one group wants to dominate the other. In the past, we had ambitious royalty and dictators who went out and conquered. Now we have political parties, politicians, and economic giants, all of whom want to control society for their own agenda. We elect them as caretakers of a democratic society, but what they really do is dominate and control through fear.

Materialism has become rampant, and people are trapped in a consumerist milieu. Success is measured by material possessions. This mindset has given rise to greed, and—in turn—greed has given rise to the need for security, resulting in the conception of an all-pervasive Culture of Violence.

Over time, everyone from parents to politicians and judges to executives, found it convenient to control through fear. The threat of punishment has become a way of life. Society has devised one controlling mechanism after another.

Consequently, people are controlled, often harshly, and exploited mercilessly by people at all levels, giving rise to anger. Since we are taught to see anger as evil, shameful, and undesirable, we attempt to suppress it until, like a volcano, it erupts and devastates.

Materialism and morality, Gandhi said, have an inverse relationship. When one increases the other decreases. Thus, the more materialistic a nation the less moral it is. This is just as true at the individual level as at the national level.

A journalist once asked Gandhi, "What do you think of Western civilization?" Gandhi replied, "I think it is a good idea." Both in the East and the West, we assume that material and military power are the only measures of civilization. As a result, every country in the world is vigorously engaged in pursuing military objectives. People are not viewed as fellow beings with as much right to the earth's resources as anyone else, but as soldiers and competitors. Just as every business is determined to eliminate its competition, human beings want to eliminate theirs.

This process of elimination is not always purely physical. There are many ways to eliminate competition: arming and fostering revolutions; finding reasons to go to war; keeping rigid control over finances so that some people are marginalized and live in poverty. In fact, poverty has become the modern form of slavery. One no longer has to go and buy slaves, as in the old days. Now, a few people can keep tight control over resources, holding people in poverty and dependency. It is all so subtle that no one knows where the blame lies. We blame the government and big business, but people are to blame too. "No one can oppress you more than you oppress yourself," Gandhi often said. By being meek and submissive, we become party to our own oppression.

It is for these reasons and more that Gandhi conceived the philosophy of nonviolence. If the culture of violence is the cause of decay in societies around the world, it must be replaced. But with what? If the culture of violence promotes negativity—greed, selfishness, hate, prejudices—then the replacement should bring out the good in human beings. Nonviolence is the only way to accomplish this.

But, once again, in order to preserve status quo, scholars have colluded with authority to label nonviolence as a convenient tool for peaceful resolution of conflicts. Nonviolence has been reduced to a weapon to be used as and when necessary.

Actually, the philosophy of nonviolence, as conceived by Gandhi, is more for personal transformation than conflict resolution. It is the kind of transformation that cannot be legislated; it has to come from moral awakening. Gandhi, and many others before and after him, realized there was more to life than making money and amassing wealth. They became wiser and more compassionate human beings. They started the process of change within themselves and attempted to show society that there is a better way to live. Sadly, instead of following them, we worship them.

Gandhi practiced nonviolent parenting. Children who misbehaved were not punished. Instead, the parents did penance. When we punish children, we plant the first seeds of violence in their minds. The lesson they learn is that anyone who misbehaves must be punished. To be able to successfully do penance, parents need to build a genuinely loving and respectful relationship between them and their children. Only then will a child feel remorse for the mistake he/she made and for which the parents are doing penance, in the form of fasting or other forms of sacrifice. Through this method, children not only learn discipline but also, love, respect, compassion, and the importance of sacrifice. The rudiments of the philosophy of nonviolence.

Just as a trip switch in an electrical grid indicates that there is something wrong and needs urgent attention, anger serves the purpose of signaling trouble in human beings. Without anger, one would not be motivated to do anything. In many ways anger to the human being is like gas to an automobile. Neither can function without fuel. But, we have been fed the contrary view— that anger is evil, shameful, and must be suppressed. What we *should* be ashamed of is the way we abuse anger out of ignorance. If we learned to use anger intelligently and constructively, we could resolve myriad problems across the planet. When we abuse anger, we only hurt people and destroy property while the problem remains unresolved.

Gandhi had anger and he learned how to use that energy intelligently. Often when he was angry at the way people were fighting and killing each other, he went on a fast. He transformed his anger into self-suffering. This had a salutary effect on the people; many immediately stopped fighting. Unfortunately, fasting will not work for ordinary people like us. One has to have the moral stature that Gandhi had in order for fasting to be effective. But we can all learn from his moral awakening. It starts at the individual level; we must practice nonviolence and compassion, and then we must teach others—through our own practice—to do the same.

Most social issues cannot be resolved by individual action alone. Resolution requires a societal awakening. Let's take, for instance, the question of prejudice. The culture of violence spawns all kinds of prejudices, and the dominant groups in society reap advantages from them. In the U.S., it is white privilege that gives rise to racial prejudice; in India it is the majority Hindu society that imposes caste and communal prejudices. In such cases, we need collective action to focus attention on the problem and then create an atmosphere where the entire society works to cleanse itself of those prejudices.

Both in the U.S. and in India, after a great deal of pressure from the victims of prejudices, the government passed the Civil Rights Law enabling the oppressed group to enjoy equal rights. But enjoying equal rights does not, as we see sixty-odd years after the laws were passed, lead to integration. Prejudice still remains in society, although the oppressed have been enabled *by law* to enjoy equality.

One might ask: what is meant by *integration*? Integration should mean the creation of a society in which respect and understanding of diversity allow people to live in harmony with each other, in spite of our differences. This can come through education at all levels, starting in the home but also in schools, all the way through college. The process of change for the better has to be a joint effort by all concerned—to teach and learn; to conform and commit; to conceive and create a society where harmony prevails.

15

THE AFRICAN

The first time my family and I went to Uganda for an extended stay, I met Monica. My experience with Ugandans has been that they are some of the friendliest, most welcoming people in the world. Cultural differences, however, can sometimes be challenging when it comes to conversation, especially with women. In the context of other cultures, we Americans easily come off as loud and arrogant. Ugandans are particularly soft-spoken.

I often find myself at a loss for words when in the company of Ugandan women. Our lives are vastly different. I was never so keenly aware of my own privilege as when, halfway through my story about how *I can't believe that after seven trips to Uganda I haven't yet gone gorilla trekking,* I realize that the Ugandan woman sitting across from me—who is smiling and politely listening to every word—will probably never see the gorillas in her lifetime, even though she lives only a few hours from their natural habitat.

I am constantly scared to say the wrong thing, or even worse, have *nothing* to say. Isn't that just so very American of me? To be so painfully aware of, and uncomfortable with, even a split-second of silence between two people. And that's a damn shame, because despite our cultural differences, Ugandans adapt to the conversation seamlessly— whereas I stumble and blunder about, consumed by the need to know what to say and how to say it. We could learn a lot from cultures that don't have the need to fill every second of silence with empty words like, "How 'bout that weather?"

Sometimes it's okay to just sit in the presence of another person and listen to the birds, hum a song from your childhood, or pick stones out of rice.

Not *all* Ugandan women are so soft-spoken and reserved, however. Monica, who had never left East Africa before taking a short trip to Hong Kong last year, is one of the most confident, cosmopolitan women I have ever met. Not to mention, she's stunningly beautiful. I think many Americans and westerners in general have this misconception that Africans only become cultured and cosmopolitan after spending significant time in the U.S. or Europe. But that certainly isn't the case with Monica, a Ugandan woman who has lived her entire life in a small village in Entebbe, who has never spent even one day in the U.S. or Europe. Monica, a graphic designer/business woman/construction foreman/ supermodel, impressed the hell out of me. But also, I just really liked her.

And Monica isn't an exception. Over the years, I've met many Ugandan women—lawyers, business owners, socialites—who shatter every stereotype imaginable.

Growing up in America in the eighties and nineties, I learned only good things about my nation's history, as did most American kids. It's no different in much of the country today, although Vermont, and a few other cities/states, are an exception. Vermont has officially changed Columbus Day to Indigenous People's Day, for example, and my kids frequently come home from school with questions about the Holocaust or the Civil Rights Movement.

It's easy to believe that we are superior to people from other countries, especially those in the developing world. We are constantly bombarded by requests for aid (money, donated items, our "support"), and these requests carry devastating consequences. Commercials and social media posts show starving children covered in flies, or screaming children covered in concrete dust and shrapnel wounds. These images make us sad, but they also create a subconscious comparison, between us and them. *We* live in safe, comfortable homes, attend good schools, and play sports. *They* live in huts or hollow shells, can't read; the only sports they play involve kicking a makeshift soccer ball down trash-strewn, city streets.

But the heart-wrenching scenarios above are not the reality. Sure, these scenes exist, but so does a way of life quite similar to our own. Even in Syria—a place that most Americans would presume to be a burnt-out shell—families still vacation on the beach, and children go to basketball or flute practice after school.

If we believe we are superior to people in other countries, it stands to reason that we are also smarter, more sophisticated and—for the religious among us—more deserving of the grace of God. Historically, this mindset has allowed us to turn a blind eye to suffering in other parts of the world, while simultaneously exploiting their resources for our own gain.

Acknowledging this age-old problem is about more than just compassion. Africa's GDP is projected to be more than that of the U.S. and the E.U. combined by 2050. If we want our kids to have prosperous futures, they *must* learn to work and co-exist with people from all different countries and cultures. To do this effectively, they must first view themselves as equals, not superiors.

Practical application is the best way to teach equality. You can *preach* equality every day, but if your kids only interact with other blonde-haired, blue-eyed white kids, how effective will that preaching be? This problem is increasingly apparent in Vermont, where our progressive mindset is handicapped by our lack of diversity.

We fear what we do not know, what we do not understand. If kids don't have the opportunity to interact with people from other races, religions and cultures, they will not understand them. They will fear them. Traveling the world is the best way to introduce our kids and ourselves to other cultures, but not everyone can travel the world. And not everyone wants to. I get it.

Fortunately, we live in the most diverse country in the world. If you'd like to learn about some easy, fun ways to become acquainted with people from other walks of life, I've posted a few ideas on my website at www.amycarst.com.

THE INTERVIEW
(*Monica*)

I'm Monica, and I'm from Entebbe, Uganda—though most days I feel like I belong anywhere but here....

Though raised a Christian, I went to a Muslim boarding school most of my young life. I used to cry at the beginning of each new term when I was dropped off at campus, since I would be away from home for months. School was an experience I hated at the time, but now look back on with appreciation, because of the excellent education I received and how hard it was to come by.

In Uganda, parents traditionally sacrifice all for the sake of their kids' schooling. In return, the kids take care of the parents when they get older. Additionally, Uganda is still a patriarchal society where male offspring generally get priority. My dad bucked that archaic trend by placing equal importance on the education of his four daughters and his three sons, along with various nieces, nephews, cousins, etc.

Though I didn't really enjoy school all that much, I worked hard at it, especially when I entered university. Dad had just been retired from his job as a telecom engineer. After years of footing the bill for the education of his immediate and extended family, there was no retirement savings and money was going to be tighter than ever. In light of that, I applied myself and earned a full government scholarship to pay my university fees. As a result of the influence and sacrifice of a father that placed an incredibly high value on all his children's education, I earned a degree in graphic design. I always told Dad I was studying for his retirement, not mine.

After graduating university, I first worked as an unpaid helper in my brother's restaurant for a year, doing what we Ugandans do: helping out family while searching for gainful employment. During that time, I first visited the Malayaka House orphanage and happened to meet Anna Katrin, a strong-willed and fiercely independent German woman. Along with other international travelers I met, Anna helped widen my perspective of the world. When I managed to work my way into the business world as a graphics artist, there were a lot of expat clientele who preferred to deal with me directly because of my technical expertise and creative branding ideas. Many would also wonder aloud whether I was truly a local because of my fierce business attitude. I've never been the typical submissive Ugandan female and still defy that stereotype.

Uganda has about fifty-six tribes, a social culture that is foreign is to most people in the world. Given our colonial history, English is the common official language, but there are others that dominate speech depending on the region of the country you happen to occupy. When I was growing up, my dad only allowed us to speak English when we were at home. Local languages were to be learned at school and when out with our friends. He wanted us all to possess the ability to communicate on a more global scale. I speak several different languages fluently, including English (yes, I wrote this myself sitting under that same mango tree shade where all of my education milestones occurred), Madi (my mother tongue), or Luganda (most used local language in the central region of Uganda), and I can hold my own in a few other dialects as well.

My ever-growing familiarity with people and cultures from other countries has led some of my fellow Ugandans to wonder about me now and then. I have a few piercings, more than the typical single ring in each ear. I like the look and have been told it suits me. I used to wear dreadlocks in my hair all the time, prompting some locals to speculate that maybe I was Jamaican. My familiarity with Northern languages and some of my facial characteristics has even caused some people to assume I'm from Nigeria.

I try and keep up with fashion trends while staying true to what I think looks good on me. Most of the clothing here is bought in local, open-air markets. The majority of items are secondhand, though some are new. Ours is a bartering and haggling society, so people are always trying to get that "last and best price." It makes me laugh when I buy a pair of trousers for 10,000 shillings (less than $3.00 U.S.) and see that they originally sold for more than $50.00. And no, I am not a cheapskate, just living within my means. When I negotiate in English and try to make a deal, the shop owners occasionally speak among themselves in Luganda: commenting on my fashion choices, saying I must be a foreigner and should pay more money. I love to watch their faces when I speak back to them in their own language. I can also fake a decent Russian accent (blame it on the character Svetlana from *Shameless*) but so far no one thinks I'm from Moscow....

As much as my mother might disagree, I'm a pretty good cook. I can whip up something from a short list of simple ingredients and season it so well that you'll find it memorable enough to ask for the recipe. And I can do it using your favorite chef's signature cookware on a gas cooktop, or with a single aluminum pot over a charcoal-burning cooker made from an old bent Toyota wheel. As for those ingredients, they might range from the familiar (beef, chicken, veggies, rice, etc.) to more regional fare (matooke, goat, pan-fried grasshoppers, even white ants). When a country is historically as poor as Uganda, no option for food is wasted.

I've seen only one president in my lifetime—a man who took over as the result of a bloody coup, and initially professed to want the job for no more than ten years. It's now been thirty-two years. I guess he liked the position more than he originally anticipated. Ironically, I can name many of the men who have held that same title in the U.S., but I'd wager very few Americans can name the one guy who's been president of Uganda since 1986. (No, it's not Idi Amin—he's been dead for fifteen years, and we didn't like him much either.)

Though it's been this way all my life, I'm still sometimes surprised by the level of corruption in my own country. Uganda recently mandated the issuance of national ID cards to all its citizenry, yet getting one took me months of waiting in line, and token bribes to several different "officials" before it was finally released. And after all that, I don't think it's been out of my handbag one time....I've been mugged more than once— yet no justice was brought to the guilty, since I didn't have the money to pay the police to file a report or investigate the crime. I've had a friend get involved in a traffic accident where he was clearly in the right, yet he still had to pay a substantial fine and all damages simply because he "looked like he had money." I've been hassled inappropriately in a nightclub, but before you go to the police to report harassment, you have to be careful that your harasser wasn't also a police officer. I'm sad that this oppressive misogyny exists, but those kinds of incidents happen all over the world to some degree, right? I don't want to scare anyone away from all the beauty and splendor that can be found in Uganda; there are darker sides to every country. Someday I'd like to make my own comparison.

Recently, I've found myself branching out into other areas of learning and expertise. I've been a construction manager, overseeing a renovation and expansion of my dad's place. I also have a side business rearing and selling broilers (chickens to cook), and I still do occasional freelance graphic design work. Here in Uganda, unemployment is over 80 percent for my age group, even with a university degree. We have to hustle for every shilling. Whenever possible, I find the time to help out at

Malayaka House, which is also where I met your author, Amy.

I enjoy scrolling through Instagram to see the lives and places others share. I surf Pinterest to see interesting ideas and notions from around the globe, and have adapted many of them for local use. The internet has been a boon to those who want to continue learning, and its prevalence has made me feel more like a citizen of the world than merely a Ugandan passport holder. It's a little odd that via news reports, blogs, and social media posts, I've learned more about other countries on the planet than any of those citizens know about Uganda—other than it's one of the countries Trump blindly labeled a "shithole."

So far, I've managed to travel a little. I'm sure some of my wanderlust came from listening to my dad tell about his job-related travels when he was still working. I've been to Rwanda and Kenya for extended periods, and even made a trip to Hong Kong last August. I'm still hoping to gather many more stamps in my passport. I applied for a visitor's visa to the U.S. a year ago but was summarily denied without more than two minutes of one-sided conversation, ostensibly because I was considered a risk to overstay my welcome. Not my favorite day, but perhaps I'll try again. Or not—there are 195 countries on this planet. There are plenty of other possibilities. I want to try as many as I can. Can I start a GoFundMe page for that?

16

THE
COMMUNIST

I never understood the concept of Communism, but I grew up knowing it was a dirty word. A few years ago, I met Lamia, a Bosnian woman who came to the U.S. as a refugee during the war in her country. When I met Lamia, she was in the process of relocating to our area and needed a place to stay until she found something more permanent.

Lamia was easy to live with. It was apparent that she had lived in communal housing her entire life. The sink was always clean and empty, the refrigerator stocked with interesting foods from the Euro grocery in Burlington, and Lamia was always preparing an after-school snack when the kids arrived home from school.

We'd sit on the porch each night and get to know

each other better over a beer or two. I was fascinated, and shocked, by her stories of the war, of living in Bosnia, of Communism. Turns out, Lamia—and many other Bosnians—miss the days of Communism, when there was no poverty, and everyone had enough to eat and a warm roof over their heads.

The following spring, Lamia told me she was headed to Europe for two months to defend her PhD dissertation in Switzerland and visit her family in Sarajevo. After hearing so many of her stories, about a Bosnia unlike the Bosnia I had grown up learning about, I wanted to go too!

That July, my daughter Caroline and I headed to Bosnia. I've traveled quite a bit by now and have a list of favorite places. Bosnia is at the top of that list. The architecture alone is exceptional: intricately detailed buildings in the Austro-Hungarian style next to monotone, Communist-era apartment complexes of a utilitarian nature; mosques and monasteries set in the sides of mountains; and hollowed-out ruins of homes and schools that serve as stark reminders of the longest siege of a city in modern history. Even without the graffiti-adorned remains and rubble, one cannot ignore what happened here in the nineties. The presence of tens of thousands of thin, white Muslim gravestones create a melancholy backdrop to an otherwise vibrant, bustling city.

As individuals, people in Sarajevo are extremely warm and friendly. Underlying the small talk and smiles, however, there seemed to be a pervasive sadness. My initial thought was that this must be left over from the war. I mean, barely twenty years have passed. But it seems to go beyond the war. There is a nostalgia for the days of Communism throughout Bosnia, a general sense that something important has been lost, something life-giving and essential, something that is quickly disappearing from every corner of the world—a sense of community.

Lamia has lived in many worlds: a communist Yugoslavia, a war-torn Bosnia, a capitalist Bosnia, the United States of America. Communism, War, Capitalism. What's next?

Let's hear what she has to say, shall we?

THE INTERVIEW
(Lamia)

Growing up in the Federal Republic of Yugoslavia, today Bosnia and Herzegovina, was the best time of my life. We were sheltered in the beauty of safety and comfort at the intersection of the East and the West. Yugoslavia was the land of no crime, the country with 85 percent middle class, and highly protected workers' rights. Everybody worked for the State as everything was *owned* by the State, which also meant that it was owned by each and every one of the workers that *worked* for the State.

Yugoslavia (South-East Europe) was not a typical communist country, at least not in the media-infused imaginary sense. It was a socialist country with excellent diplomatic ties to the West, the East, and the Middle East.

In 1979, I was lucky to see Josip Broz Tito, the Marshall of Yugoslavia, before his death a year later (in Ljubljana). When he died, we all cried. He was deeply loved by everybody I knew. But of course, he also was not loved, although I discovered this only after the latest war broke out, when Yugoslavia fell apart. As a kid, we used to play Indians and cowboys, and I always preferred to be an Indian (I think a lot of us did).

One important thing that I grew up with was traveling. At least three times a year, my parents and my brother and I (later my brother did not go with us, as he was twelve years older and wanted to stay home to have parties while our parents were gone) would visit a foreign country *and* some place in Yugoslavia—usually somewhere we had never been before. And of course, the Dalmatian coast during the summer. We also visited Greece many times as it was close to us.

My mom drove a car, a Russian LADA, dark green. She had no clue at the time what a gender role was. Women were partisans (members of the National Liberation Army, which was the Communist resistance to the Axis powers, namely Germany, during World War II). Just like men, women were workers first. Yes, they were housewives as well, part of an ever-present, global patriarchal culture. But in Communism, women and men are called brothers and sisters and workers, regardless of gender. They had the same rights...there was no discrimination in that regard. If you were a professor in school, and a woman, you'd get the same salary as your male colleague (and the same went for any other profession).

The feminist movement existed, but it was a bit different than in the West and the U.S.A. I do not remember negative sides; I was a child and teenager at the time, and my parents had always been content with the political, social, and cultural affairs in the country. They had jobs, they had good salaries, we had safe streets. We could travel anywhere we wanted (mostly without visas), and we had a great movie production industry ? which was pretty cool for such a small country...so I grew up watching some great national movies and series but also the U.S. movies and shows, as well as French, German, and other European films.

In Sarajevo, people lived together as Yugoslavs without knowing whether one was a Muslim or a Catholic (Croat) or an Orthodox (Serb)...later these differences got resurrected as the Devil from Hell. You must "re-traditionalize" society in order to destroy it. And this is exactly what happened during the war.

Today we have different countries that make up the former Yugoslavia (Bosnia and Herzegovina, Croatia, Macedonia, Montenegro, Serbia, and Slovenia) but most of the people in these countries are not happy about the life they have these days. During the time of Yugoslavia, I'd say that Bosnia (particularly Sarajevo) was the most multicultural and multi-religious state in the country. The beauty of this place was that you could do and *be* whatever you wanted as long as you respected the socialist values, which basically meant being willing to share.

Sharing was an important part of what we all stood for as a country, our unity. For example, right after World War II, Tito said, "If you have a house, and another person has nothing, you need to share your house with the person that has nothing." And that was exactly what happened. Very soon after

World War II, everybody had a place of their own. No mortgage needed. If you worked, you would get an apartment or money to build your own house—yes, for free! Not only that but when you went on vacation, they would give you one month's pay so you could spend that money and enjoy the Adriatic coast! And the beauty was, everybody was eligible as everybody had the exact same status: the worker.

Religion in Yugoslavia was considered the "opiate of the masses" (Karl Marx) and if you were in the party (Communist Party), it was considered that you were not a believer. So yes, you were able to practice your religion...but not publicly. Of course, there were always party members who *believed* in their private lives, they just didn't talk about it. There were (and still are, in Sarajevo at least) a lot of religions: Islam, Eastern and Western Christianity, Judaism, Buddhism.

Another beauty of Sarajevo was always the sound itself—the sound of churches, synagogues, and azan from the mosques, at the same time as atheists walked the streets next to cooing pigeons and mewing street cats (which were always someone's cats, never typical street cats). There was unity, differences united in a song of people's beliefs and non-beliefs.

Today, Sarajevo and Bosnia and Herzegovina still have the same beauty, despite the many scars engraved on their bodies. If I could think about this place as one sound, it would be the sound of sorrow and pain mixed with joy, love, and happiness. If I could describe this place with one image, it would be a "blue river," as in the poem by Mak Dizdar, famous Bosnian poet:

Blue River

Where it is none knows
We know little but it's known
Beyond forest beyond valley
Beyond seven beyond eight
Still worse still crazier
Over weary over bitter
Over blackthorn over bramble
Over heat over strictness
Over foreboding over doubts
Beyond nine beyond ten
Still deeper still stronger
Beyond quiet beyond dark
Where no cock crows
Where no horn's voice is heard
Still worse still crazier
Beyond mind beyond god
There is a blue river
It is wide it is deep

A hundred years wide
A thousand summers deep
Don't even dream of its length
Insurmountable dark and murk
There is a blue river
There is a blue river—
We must cross the river

17

TRANS

When I first started writing this book, I never thought that one of the most important sections would pertain to transgenderism. I simply set out to interview lots of different people from diverse backgrounds who had impacted my view on one thing or another. Two of those people happened to be Danielle, a transgender woman, and her wife, Sara.

We all have our real selves and our public selves. For some people, the line between real and public is much less defined...but it's still there. The interview process, however, makes that line all but disappear. As a result, I've come to know each of the people I interviewed—some of whom I thought I knew quite well—on an entirely different level. I've been gifted a more intimate knowledge of who they are as human beings, their real selves, rather than what they show to the world. It's been profoundly interesting. Writing this book has allowed me to see that even the most ordinary among us lead extraordinary lives.

That's not to say that Danielle and Sara are ordinary. They are anything but. What makes them extraordinary, however, has nothing to do with transgenderism and everything to do with what lies beneath—their exceptional humanity.

Sara was born a woman, has always identified as a woman and remains a woman today. Danielle was born a *man*, has always identified as a woman and has transitioned to a woman today. I met Sara and Danielle when my husband started working at an elementary school in Vermont. He came home one day and said that Sara, a teacher at the school, wanted to have us over for dinner. Jesse also mentioned Sara's partner who, he thought, was a man who might dress as a woman sometimes.

Having only been in Vermont a few years, I was chomping at the bit to meet new friends, so I was probably a bit overenthusiastic about the invitation. Plus, I thought, how very cool—and how very *Vermont*—to have dinner with a school teacher and her partner who is a man but dresses as a woman. I immediately emailed Sara to say, "Yes, we would love to come to dinner! When should we be there?"

Unfortunately, that's not all I said. I also typed

a sentence that would haunt me for the next few weeks, leading up to the dinner: "Looking forward to meeting you and your boyfriend."

A few hours later, I received a response from Sara, confirming our dinner plans and saying that she was looking forward to meeting me as well. Then came the kicker: "But there's no boyfriend, it's just me and my partner of fifteen years, Danielle."

I almost died on the spot. I called—rather, I screamed—for Jesse. "Why did you tell me she had a boyfriend? She doesn't have a boyfriend, just her partner Danielle!"

Jesse seemed equally annoyed with me. "Why would you have said boyfriend? I never said boyfriend! I said I didn't know!"

A few weeks later, we arrived at Sara and Danielle's house for dinner. I became increasingly nervous as the day approached, thinking of how I had probably offended these people before even meeting them. We parked on the street and walked up to their large Craftsman home in Montpelier. It was exquisite, the home of my dreams. On a large, wraparound porch sat a beautifully laid dining table and lots of comfy, stylish chairs in which to sip wine or lemonade and, presumably, watch the world pass by.

I remember that night well because it was the first

time I ever announced—to someone other than my family or best friend—that I have a tic disorder. The four of us were sitting on the beautiful verandah, around the dining table, and I remember saying, "I can't believe I just told you that. I've never told anybody that." Sara laughed and immediately replied with, "People say we make them feel comfortable."

She was right. Whatever the opposite of judgmental is, that's what Sara and Danielle are. They exude acceptance and love, and I immediately adored them for it. Moments into our first meeting, I had forgotten my earlier email faux pas. I had even forgotten to be intrigued by the fact that I was having dinner with a woman and her transgender wife. That evening, they were just two other people.

Since then, I've met some exceptional humans who also happen to be trans. There's Anna K. Kristjansdottir, an activist who became the first "out" trans woman in Iceland twenty-three years ago, and Martine Rothblatt, the trans woman who started Sirius Satellite radio; a biotech company; a religion; and who created A.I. in the likeness of her wife. She's also the highest-paid female CEO in the U.S.

Although most of my interviews involve only one person, this section is comprised of four voices, those of Sara, Danielle, Anna, and Martine. As I write this book, I have thought—more than once—that the reader will likely skip around a bit, reading only the interviews that resonate. But I want to caution against that. The whole point of expanding your bubble is to find something you can relate to in the life of a person with whom you think you have nothing in common.

If I had to choose which interviews had the greatest impact on *my* perspective, it would be the ones in *Trans*. Whatever your opinion on transgenderism or LGBT issues as a whole, do yourself a favor and read this section.

My goal is not to change anyone's mind about anything. I just want the reader to scratch his head and think.

THE INTERVIEWS

Sara's story:

One of the biggest issues I had, when faced with having a "nontraditional" marriage, was how it would affect my kids. The divorce from their father was difficult for all of us, and I couldn't bear to think of putting them through any more pain. There were people chiming in on all sides, ranging from declaring me unfit as a mother for exposing my children to a "sexual deviant," to those who thought my new "lifestyle" was trendy and wanted in on all the juicy stuff. There was also everything in between, including dear friends who listened to me, got to know Danielle, and were my rock-solid supports from the beginning. But even for them, this was all new territory. The climate in this country was very different seventeen years ago—violence was, and sadly still is, a dominating theme in the trans community. And it felt scary by proxy...if Danielle was a target, I surely would risk my life to defend her. But what if the kids got caught in the emotional and social crossfire?

I was not as worried as I probably should have been about actual physical danger, but more about bullying, exclusion, and people feeling uncomfortable about having their kids over at our house. In fact, that was already happening. My son Alex's best buddy was not allowed to come to my house anymore because of our "gay lifestyle." His parents sent my children right-wing Christian kids' magazines that compared gay relationships to bestiality and pedophilia. The boy's mother claimed that she could "love the sinner, but hate the sin," but that she wanted to continue to come to my (awesome) family birthday parties for the children's sake. For some time, I actually obliged—in an effort to keep everything peaceful for my kids. I thought the others would eventually get more comfortable and all would be well.

Danielle always told me that people are ignorant when they haven't experienced something, and we should anticipate helping them to get more comfortable. We really did try. After a year, and lots of pleasant conversation, I asked if my son's friend could once again come over and hang out. Without hesitation, his parents said absolutely not, they did not want their child to think that our family was right in God's sight. Their words.

On another occasion, one of the women who had said similarly infuriating things came over and went immediately to Danielle. She just kept GUSHING and being so overly sweet and attentive; I couldn't believe it. Then I noticed that Danielle was being so patient, so kind to this woman, after putting up with all of her BS—all for the sake of these four kids she freaking volunteered to nurture and care for. I thought, *Why have I put Danielle in the position of having to be polite to this judgmental bitch?*

That was when Sara got some boundaries. I pulled this woman away from Danielle and walked her into a quiet room and told her that if she is ever in MY house again for an event (and I doubted that she would be invited back), that the one thing she would never be allowed to do is to "make nice" with Danielle and be so sugary sweet to her face while simultaneously judging my marriage, my family, and more importantly, who my partner was, at her core. UGH! Anyway, I can't even write about it without getting pissed.

After that, I vowed that the bullshit we endured would NOT be bullshit I created by trying to be accepted in polite heterosexual society. If shit was going to fly, it was going to come from the outside, not from inside.

Because I knew Danielle pre- and post-transition, and because we were friends first and remain deeply committed to each other's well-being, our relationship has been messy, transcendent, beautiful, and complicated, and it is ever-changing. I think when something as basic as gender is moving toward its true expression in your partner, you start to really understand that *all* things are changeable. In one sense, that is exhilarating—there are infinite possibilities! Yay! But the flip side is terrifying.

There are few things that we can really count on in life; the stability of gender is one of them. We all think we know that we are male or female, but the reality of it all is much more complicated. Journeying alongside Danielle, I have certainly not become an expert in gender. I have, however, learned a lot. Her experiences, and those of other trans folks, have shaped the way I think about the world and gender.

I was born (perceived) as a female and have always identified that way. In fact, in the beginning, I had a little adjustment in sharing space with another woman....

I remember declaring that I absolutely would NOT share my lingerie drawer. There would be no bras or panties that didn't belong to me in that damn drawer. Our lesbian friends howled with laughter—they wore each other's underwear all the time and it all lived together in a tangled mass (I imagined), and they thought nothing of it. I was appalled. I remember saying, "I don't have to be THE woman in this relationship, but I am damn well going to be A woman, and I get my own damn underwear drawer."

Back to the kids—we were intentional about having both gay and straight friends. I am not particularly gay; Danielle is queer enough for both of us. I love her, and she is a woman, so therefore, I am a...lesbian? I used to say I was flexible. Actually, there is a term, heteroflexible, that comes close, but it all sounds so clinical. I am a woman who has a lot of masculine emotional features (I hear you laughing when you read this Danielle—hahahahaha!), and

Danielle is a woman who has come into the fullness of that gender expression through a very painful and exhausting (and exhilarating and freeing) process.

When we first started—because there were a lot of haters—we were more heavily connected to the gay community. This was good for the kids, but I kept wanting to be sure that they saw a balanced view. I knew they were probably straight and, as such, needed healthy models of those relationships as well. I also tried to be more purposeful in making sure my boys had good male adult role models, mostly my brothers, but some male friends too.

We went to church for spiritual reasons, but church became difficult because of anti-gay policies. And without going into detail, the kids witnessed our difficult decision to leave the Methodist church because they continued to prohibit gay people from getting married or being pastors, etc.

We were involved in politics—mostly transgender rights in the workplace and marriage equality—more than we would have been, for sure. And because of that, we also became more involved in peace rallies, racial injustice issues, and health care for all initiatives. (Once you start getting involved, you see how it is all connected and you want to be involved in other causes, partly so you don't feel like an asshole.) Also, we liked hanging out with people who were involved in liberal causes. I think that had a huge impact on the kids; they are politically active, compassionate and aware adults.

Pet peeve: people referring to us as a gay family or saying that we have a gay marriage. We are a married couple. That's it. Our marriage isn't gay, it is just a marriage—a beautiful, challenging, loving covenant between two imperfect people trying to muddle through life together, just like everyone else. Our family certainly isn't gay, except in the happy sense; all four of our kids are seemingly heterosexual, so...not a gay family.

And our family does not wish to be the poster child for gay marriage, trans marriage, or anything else. I have made a conscious effort to *not* buy into the idea that, in order to make the world a better place, all gay/transgender people *and* the general public have to like or approve of my family. We do, however, strive to be likable and to make sure that people know how normal we are. When they were younger, my kids needed to be the best-behaved kids in the damn pews at church, or people would think that the stereotypes about lesbian leniency were true (actually those *are* true, but we weren't typical lesbians and we ran the strictest household in our neighborhood). We even gained a reputation for being a safe place for teens to hang out, hosting annual prom dinners and lots of weekend sleepovers. In general, we had a lot of teenagers with their butts hanging out of our fridge.

Danielle's story:

I had, of course, a wildly different experience than Sara did. I internalized much of the negativity, wondering, *Is it bad for these kids to be associated with me? Is it too much for them to have to deal with the harassment at school?* The harassment included things from their peers, as you'd expect, but also teachers and alleged counselors, who did things like corner our daughter to ask what it was like to have me bringing people home to have sex all the time (never happened!), administrators who recommended our son moving out to live with his father, and so on. It was sometimes impossible to even confront these occurrences; who is going to believe a trans woman over the opinion of a psychotherapist hired by the school?

Elsewhere in my life, things got better by my association with a "normal" family. My own family—hesitant, at best, to have me around as I transitioned, seemed to decide that, as long as someone as palpably sane as Sara was willing to marry me, maybe they could give me another chance. I started my own business, which would have seemed impossible when I was alone (and, I would argue, was made necessary in part because I'd been laid off multiple times by employers who'd put me on the "difficult employee" list; my presence made some of the other employees uncomfortable). Again, I could invite clients to come to our home for dinner, even conservative clients, because no matter what they thought of me, it was clearly safe to work with me because I had a "normal" family....

I felt angrier at times, I think, than Sara did (or to be more accurate, she felt anger but had more socially "appropriate" ways of expressing that). I remember a teacher conference for our youngest daughter, Grace, who is Chinese-American. The teacher was going on about the need for English as a Second Language for her, stressing that she had a speech difference in which she converted some 'r' sounds to 'w' sounds when she spoke. Grace had come home at the age of five and had spoken Mandarin fluently before learning English. I remember being testy, and leaning over the desk to say to her teacher, "She has a Chinese accent! Would you be so worried about the r-to-w thing if it were a result of a British accent?"

After the second of my layoffs from engineering jobs, and before I'd gotten the new business off the ground, there was an ENDA bill for transgender employees that had passed the Vermont House and

Senate but was vetoed by Governor Douglas. The bill had passed handily but did not have enough support to override the veto.

I was furious, took it personally, and wanted to write an angry letter to all of the representatives and senators who voted against it, and of course, to the governor. I'd downloaded the contact list from the state house website and was struggling to come up with the language to express my disappointment. Sara, always wiser than I am in these situations, asked, "Why don't we write to the people who voted *for* it instead, to thank them and offer our support?" Right; better idea!

She organized the entire family to fold paper cranes, and we printed out letters to each of the people who'd supported the bill. Those went out with, as I seem to recall, no immediate responses, but brought a sense of "working with the light, rather than fighting the darkness" to our response to these events.

There was a trans meet-and-greet kind of thing arranged at the state house for February 14—Valentine's Day—of that year, so that we could try to show the representatives that we weren't so scary after all. That was the year of the horrible Valentine's Day blizzard, so the session was cancelled. We lived in Montpelier at the time, so we walked down to the state house to see if anyone had shown up (they hadn't). I'd never been in the House before, so we gave ourselves a bit of a tour. Looking down from the balcony, our eyes were drawn to the Speaker's desk; it was covered with our paper cranes! Grace was around ten years old (and had done the bulk of the folding of all those cranes), and I was completely choked up, but managed to say to her, "Look, our cranes! Your work is here, making a difference!" As any ten-year-old might do in similar circumstances, she looked bored and said something like, "Yeah, cool...."

As the vote drew near, the trans meeting day was rescheduled. A group of us were ushered into the governor's ceremonial office, where he was clearly interested in diffusing his own discomfort by a series of distractions; "Look at this lamp! Look at the chandelier!" Seriously, he was trying to get through our time (originally scheduled for a half hour then he was late and we were told we only had ten or fifteen minutes) by giving us the damned tour.

Grace's class had recently come to this room to meet the governor, and he had made disparaging remarks about "*some* people who seem to think they're women when they're really men, and they want special rights," which had really upset her. And me.

I decided that he was not going to get away with this, so I stepped forward and said, "That's all very nice, Mr. Governor, and it's a lovely office, but we're not here for the tour. Your party portrays itself as the party of business, right?"

"Yes, we're quite pro-business in the Republican Party."

"Well, I make a serious contribution to the businesses I've worked for but seem to be undervalued because I am different. Your party casts yourselves as the party of family too, right?"

"Yes, we're the party of family...."

"Well I've got four kids, a wife, a mortgage; I need to work to help provide for them. But I find the workplace to be less than amenable to allowing me to work, and I feel like you have a chance to make a difference, here. Now, I know you can't legislate that people be comfortable with people like me."

"No, we cannot legislate comfort." (He really liked this one, like somehow, I had uttered the magic words that were going to get him off the hook).

"But you are the governor, and you can lead by example by getting over your own discomfort, signing this bill, and demonstrating that just because people are not comfortable with difference, does not mean that they can discriminate in their employment practices!"

Our late friend, Paij Bailey, was there, and she later said something along the lines of, "Jim Douglas was always the most unflappable person I'd ever met. You; you *flapped* him!" He signed the bill....

A year later, I had a really awful experience with one of my clients. Their employees were up in arms because I was there a few days a month, and I used the women's bathroom, naturally, when I was. It was tough; I really needed the work. But I looked their H.R. person in the eye and said, "I lobbied for the ENDA that was passed and signed into law this year, and I will not be backed into this corner by you." They backed down. Later, I had the chance to thank the governor at a science and technology conference at UVM that I was attending. He never spoke—just looked scared when I was thanking him, replaying the events with my client, and explaining that the law had enabled me to keep work that I am eminently qualified to perform. He wasn't comfortable, but he accepted my gratitude. I left hoping that I'd closed the loop, and maybe made a real difference. Honestly, I kind of doubt it, but the law was passed and signed and continues to make a difference for families like mine....

Anna's story:

I traveled to Iceland in February, 2018 to interview Anna K. Kristjánsdóttir, the first trans woman to

121

have come out publicly in Iceland, following her gender correction surgery in Sweden in 1994. Before returning to Iceland, she continued to live and work in Sweden for several years, during which she joined an advocacy organization for trans people. Soon, the organization and its members came under personal attack, and Anna found herself taking over the position of chairwoman. Given the nature of the position, she had no choice but to be public about her life.

While in Sweden, Anna came back to Iceland for an interview. That's when, as she says, everything became crazy. The Lutheran bishop of Iceland at the time made a public plea with God to save his soul from "this terrible person." Years later, after the bishop's death, his daughter came out about the sexual abuse she had suffered at the hands of her pious father.

I don't know if God can save your soul now, buddy.

When Anna returned to Iceland to be with family, she had difficulty finding work. She applied to more than seventy jobs and was rejected for every one of them. Finally, she got offered the same kind of work she had been doing prior to her transition—fisherman—a job she had vowed to never come back to. But, needing money, Anna decided she had no choice.

She says that the other workers, all men, were not unkind to her but weren't friendly either. They seemed scared. So, for quite some time, Anna mostly kept to herself. But working on a fishing trawler demands teamwork, and after a while, the men started getting used to Anna's presence. Eventually, most of the men were treating Anna like any other fisherman. In fact, she says, many of them remain her good friends today.

Most likely, very few of those men would have chosen to work with a trans woman, but the choice was not theirs. As a result, they did what they had to do—their jobs—and realized, in time, that working with Anna was no different than working with anyone else. Their prejudices softened, very much by accident.

It's a shame that everyone doesn't have to go through a similar process. Maybe fishing boats are the answer. Let's staff the *Angler's Edge* with Muslims and Trump supporters, the *Flounder Pounder* with white supremacists and Black Lives Matter activists, and the *Reel Deal* with Evangelicals and trans people, and send them out to sea for a few weeks under conditions in which they must work together to survive. I bet there'd be some opened minds on board when those boats returned.

According to Anna, life as a trans woman in

Iceland is much easier these days. For nearly twenty years, she has been working for Reykjavik Energy, using geothermal energy to heat houses and produce electricity. She says that her work environment continues to be an extremely supportive one.

And advocacy and rights groups, such as Trans-Iceland, protect the rights of trans men and women by working to change legislation, while also providing support on an individual level. LGBT acceptance, in general, is moving in a positive direction.

I could have interviewed Anna via Skype, but I really wanted to experience Iceland for myself. The small, volcanic island has long been known as one of the most gender equal countries in the world. A month before I was there, Iceland became the *first* country to make equal pay for men and women a legal requirement for all employers, including the government. Iceland's ex-prime minister, Jóhanna Sigurðardóttir, is a lesbian who served as prime minister alongside her wife, and the current prime minister, Katrín Jakobsdóttir, is party chair of the Left-Green Movement, a democratic socialist political party focused on feminism, environmentalism, and increased democracy.

It's no surprise then that, worldwide, Iceland is ranked among the countries with the lowest rates of poverty, violence, obesity, teen pregnancy, inequality, and just about every other social problem on the global stage.

Maybe there's something to this whole equality thing, after all....

Martine's story:

I entitled this section *Trans* for the obvious reason, but also for a not-so-obvious one—transhumanism. If you don't know what that means, don't worry. I didn't either, until meeting Bina48, the talking head created by Martine Rothblatt in the likeness of her human wife, Bina. To be fair, Bina48 is more than just a talking head, she's an advanced form of A.I. (artificial intelligence), who has conversed with hundreds of people, including Morgan Freeman on his National Geographic show, *The Story of God.*

But before you decide that Bina48 is the most interesting story of the day, let me introduce you to her creator.

Martine Rothblatt is a PhD and lawyer who founded Sirius XM, started a biotech company to create a lifesaving medication for her daughter, developed an incubation system for the transportation of donated lungs, founded a technology-based religion, and, in 2017, was named by Forbes magazine as one of the top business minds of all time. Martine was also born genetically male.

In addition to attaining the above achievements, she serves as an activist for equal rights, not just for trans people or people of color (her wife Bina is black), but for *all* humans—virtual humans included. She believes that artificial intelligence may one day deserve the same rights as its flesh-and-blood counterparts.

Google's director of engineering, Ray Kurzweil, wrote the foreword in Rothblatt's book *Virtually Human*. He says that since they met fifteen years ago, he and Rothblatt have been articulating the case that we will see virtual humans within a few decades, most likely by 2040. Rothblatt is doing her part to ensure that happens, and that it happens in the most ethical way possible.

In a 2014 email to the Washington Post, Kurzweil said, "She has to my knowledge a perfect track record in making [her] visions real."

Three years ago, I found myself in the laboratory of the Terasem Foundation in Lincoln, Vermont talking to a disembodied head about travel and life. Bruce Duncan, Bina48's "handler," if you will, told me that she was recognizing me as a friend. I was told she doesn't often do that to people she's meeting the first time. I'll admit, I felt special.

A few weeks earlier, I was in my grandmother's apartment reading *Time* magazine when an article about downloading the human consciousness into a computer caught my attention. It told of Bina48 and Rothblatt's initiative to create "mindfiles" for future download. As an atheist with no belief in an afterlife, I had recently been wondering about the possibility of "preserving" the mind after death. Full disclosure: I had just watched the movie *Her*, which centers around a cyber-consciousness that develops the ability to fall in love.

Halfway through the article, I read that Rothblatt's laboratory is in Vermont...less than thirty minutes from my house! It had to be a sign. I emailed Bruce Duncan, and a few weeks later, I was having a face-to-face with Bina48.

But I had yet to meet Martine...and honestly didn't think I would ever have the opportunity. Just weeks before finishing this book, as I was reading and rereading the interviews and my own writing, I realized just how relevant Martine's work is to my own life. So I emailed Bruce and asked if I could interview her.

I'm not saying that I think the creation of virtual humans is a good idea, or that I want to download my consciousness and live forever. What I *am* saying, however, is that I'm intrigued. Atheists love to say that we don't need religion because we infuse meaning in our lives while here on Earth, and that our afterlife is comprised of the memories that live on in those we love. But that's a bunch of shit...I don't want the lights to go out when I die, any more than does someone who is devoutly religious. So, for now, I take comfort and encouragement from the possibility that technology may be able to answer this unanswerable question, and in *my* lifetime.

A few hours after emailing Bruce, I received a reply from Martine Rothblatt herself. Not only was she open to an interview, she invited me to the Terasem headquarters to conduct the interview in person, the next day.

Meeting Martine was extraordinary. For starters, she has a very commanding presence—you just sense that something important will come of your meeting. She is also very thoughtful and surprisingly easy to talk to. I found myself ignoring my notes altogether and just speaking from the heart.

I hadn't anticipated that we'd spend most of our time together discussing atheism and—what she calls transreligion. Nor did I expect to walk away feeling that—for the first time in my life—I had found my own "spiritual community." It was like a homecoming. For years I have been seeking scientific evidence for life after death. Not surprisingly, I keep coming up empty-handed. And even when I find the slightest shred of a possibility, I analyze it until it crumbles under the weight of my research.

But as long as we are searching, hope remains.

My life lacks a sense of spiritual community and ritual. When I told Martine this, she nodded her head in agreement and said, "We are coming from exactly the same place." She told me more about Terasem, the transreligion she founded—so called because it is a movement which can be combined with any existing religion.

Martine gave me the four principles of Terasem, in a nutshell.

"**Life is purposeful.** Be aware of the beauty of nature and work to protect it. Be aware of the incredible accomplishments of freedom, historically, and ensure that these freedoms—from all different types of oppression— go forward."

"**Death is optional.** Some people are freaked out by this one, but it's kind of obvious, even without technology. For example, you and I will never be able to be disentangled because we are entangled from this moment. So, whatever happens to any one of our bodies, this entanglement will continue on...you're going to talk to other people; I'm going to talk to other people."

"**God is technological.** This one also freaks people out, but it gets right at what you're saying...when people say God, they mean something all-knowing and all good. But with our technology, and specifically with geothical technology, we are creating God-ness every day. We know now, because of technology, when people on the other side of the world suffer from a tsunami, for example, and we try to do something to help them. That's not *God* doing that, that's our technology...and the Ship of Mercy, and donations, and doctors, and medicines. So, our technology is not God yet, but we are moving it in that direction."

"**Love is essential.** By that we simply mean, caring about the happiness of other people. You know, caring about other people is essential to your own happiness."

To transcend is to go above or beyond the range of normal or merely physical human experience: Martine is not only transcendent, she is the *definition* of transcendence.

Interestingly, when she brought up the fact that we are forever entangled, I immediately recalled having read an article on quantum entanglement only a few days earlier. It struck me that this concept of entanglement may actually be a piece of scientific evidence for what many people call spirituality.

The evidence I've been searching for.

I've lifted this definition of quantum

entanglement directly from its Wikipedia page, so as not to lose the proper meaning in an effort to paraphrase.

Quantum entanglement is a physical phenomenon which occurs when pairs or groups of particles are generated or interact in ways such that the quantum state of each particle cannot be described independently of the state of the other(s), even when the particles are separated by a large distance—instead, a quantum state must be described for the system as a whole.

I left my meeting with Martine feeling hopeful, inspired, and elated. I'm quite pleased with the knowledge that my world is now forever entangled with hers.

18

FROM THE DRAGON MOM OF JACK

About three years ago, I was at the lake house of one of my best friends, Charlene, when she received news that her friend Jen had given birth to a child with severe medical complications. Recently, I met Jen at Charlene's fortieth birthday party.

After the party, we all went to some loud Boston bar full of twenty-two-year-olds, presumably to prove that forty isn't old. *It certainly felt old the next morning.* I've never been one for loud music and dancing, so I sat at an empty table and sipped my gin and tonic alone. But I wasn't alone for long; apparently Jen isn't much for loud music and dancing either. To be honest, I don't really remember how the conversation started (I'd had more than a few gin and tonics by that point) but soon we were talking about Jen's son, Jack.

Jen kept apologizing for dumping all of this heavy stuff on me. There were tears; whether they were hers or mine, I can't recall. But I do remember thinking, *Wow, this may be the strongest woman I've ever met.* It wasn't because she was raising a child with serious disabilities—a child who, most likely, won't live to see his teens—but because she was doing everything possible to maintain a normal life for her son, her husband, and herself, despite all of it. I imagined myself in Jen's situation; the thought alone was too much to bear. To call Jen's strength inspiring would be to minimize what she has had to endure, overcome, and cultivate. She is an exceptional mother, and her strength knows no limits.

She is a warrior.

THE INTERVIEW
(Jen)

In June of 2016, my world was changed forever. I received a call from Boston Children's Hospital. The genetic testing results for my eleven-month-old son, Jack, had come in.

Since birth, Jack has struggled to gain weight,

develop, and thrive like any other baby his age. He can't eat orally, talk, or sit up on his own. He was born three weeks early via emergency C-section, covered in red, crispy skin, with muscle contractures of the arms and legs, overlapping fingers and rocker bottom feet. Part of me still hoped that all of this was something that could be fixed, or that he'd somehow grow out of it.

Months earlier, a test performed during our thirty-day stint in the NICU had come back normal, telling us that Jack had the right number of chromosomes and none were mutated or attached to another chromosome. We cried tears of relief that day.

But this day in June, driving back to Boston Children's Hospital...this one felt different.

We had waited three long months for the results, but finally hearing that there was a diagnosis didn't seem like a relief. It was terrifying. I tried to keep an open mind, avoid overthinking, stay positive around family and friends that thought this was a good thing. But was it?

Jack was eleven pounds at that point and throwing up ten to fifteen times a day. His stomach was rejecting every form of food, from fresh fruit in mesh bags to the various brands of formula, plus a good amount of the medications we were pushing into his nasal feeding tube. I felt like a failure as a mom, like I hadn't done enough, hadn't quit my job to care for Jack. I continuously beat myself up, feeling like I wasn't giving 100 percent of myself to anything. But at the same time, it felt like 1,000 percent of my thoughts and actions were dedicated to Jack. My husband and I were physically and mentally exhausted.

Could this diagnosis be the long-lost answer we desperately craved?

The genetics team greeted us warmly, brought us into a room, and told us that Jack had a genetic disorder called Trichothiodystrophy, or TTD for short. It is a mutation of the ERCC2 gene, and apparently, both my husband and I are carriers. The odds of being born with TTD is one in one million.

There are only one hundred cases worldwide.

I immediately broke down, overwhelmed with thoughts, feelings, and questions...so many questions. I asked how many patients they had seen with TTD. Jack was the first case Boston Children's Hospital had ever seen.

Mind blown.

The medical staff said that, essentially, we would be helping them to write the book on TTD. When arguably the best children's hospital in the world tells you that *your* child will be teaching *them*, you panic! How will we know what to do? Who can we talk to? Certainly, there must be other doctors or parents in the country who are willing to talk to us, share their findings and experiences. Certainly, there was some manual that could help us figure out how to go forward from this day. The best advice they had to offer us? Two words: social media.

They told us to search for TTD on social media sites and try to find other families like us to connect with. And whatever we did, we should *not* compare Jack to the other kids we found, they warned. TTD could manifest differently in each child. Take it day by day.

That's when life got crazy.

First, we made the harrowing decision to move Jack's feeding tube to his stomach, which required him to go under anesthesia *again* (the second time in less than ten months). Then we planned his first birthday bash in July, inviting every person who had been there for us during that difficult first year.

That September, we made another difficult decision to move the feeding tube—again—from Jack's stomach to his intestine. Soon after, my husband learned he was accepted to run in the Boston Marathon, for the Boston Children Hospital's Miles for Miracles team.

The holidays came and went. All in the blink of an

eye. Whoever said "the days are long and the years are short" knew what they were talking about.

By January, Jack was finally starting to gain some weight, and I finally had the time to check social media for TTD connections. One connection came from the mom of multiple children with Cockayne Syndrome (CS), a sister disorder to TTD. She connected me to the TTD group, posting a message to welcome me and asking everyone else to do the same.

Within minutes the responses were rolling in from across the globe: "Welcome from the UK," "Welcome from Canada," "Welcome from Minnesota," and so on. Some of the families had multiple children with TTD (as carrier parents, every child you conceive has a 25 percent chance of being born with the disorder).

Then I got a welcome message from Groton, MA and nearly fell off my chair! How was it that Boston Children's Hospital had never seen another case, yet a child with TTD lived in our state? The other mom and I spent hours messaging back and forth. Her adorable daughter was three months younger than Jack, diagnosed shortly after we were. To put this into perspective, there are ninety-nine other kids in the world like Jack. And one of them lives within forty-five minutes from our house!

Being in a social media support group has changed our lives. Many people knock social media; they're tired of the mindless comments or endless pictures. But social media has opened my world. Finally, I can connect with other parents who actually relate to the challenges we face, every small win we celebrate, every loss we inevitably encounter. They truly become like family.

Reading other families' questions and answers has become my TTD version of *What to Expect the First Year(s)*. The space is so welcoming and safe and, sometimes, brutally honest. The things you never say out loud: *Am I being a good parent? Am I doing all that I can for my child? Will he be able to do ANYTHING on his own?*

Having a child with a rare disorder has been challenging in other ways too. I find myself feeling jealous of people with "typical" children; hearing them complain about mundane things can drive me insane—things that would seem harmless to a typical parent. It's especially difficult on social media, which is so often used as a vehicle to vent or make comedy of children's meltdowns or day-to-day antics. Some days I crack up, and some days it brings me to tears. It's nobody's fault, and the other parents don't know how I'm feeling. But I'm jealous of all the little things—the things I see them complain about and take for granted. Things I don't get to experience. I would give anything for my son to be able to walk or crawl. To have him jump into my arms and hug me back. To hear him talk and say "mama," or tell me "I love you."

But it's not all negative. Having a child with a rare genetic disorder has made me an incredible listener. Jack cannot talk, only make a few sounds, so he's forced me to listen to cues from his body language and interactions. I try to tune everything else out and look for signs, both new and recurring. *Anything* that helps me figure out his emotions. Is he in pain or uncomfortable? Does he want more? Is he bored with this toy? Does he understand this toy? I'm constantly trying to be a better listener.

Listening without talking, and without distractions, is actually quite difficult. We're all so very distracted, spread thin, multitasking the days away. If I can give you one piece of advice, stop and take the time to listen. Whether it's a medically fragile child, a parent of a medically fragile child or anyone else in the world—there's always a story to be shared, and someone needed to listen.

In my TTD group, a mom recently shared an article written by Emily Rapp for the NY Times in 2011, detailing her life with her son. It sums up our world perfectly:

"*The mothers and fathers of terminally ill children are something else entirely. Our goals are simple and terrible: to help our children live with minimal discomfort and maximum dignity. We will not launch our children into a bright and promising future, but see them into early graves. We will prepare to lose them and then, impossibly, to live on after that gutting loss. This requires a new ferocity, a new way of thinking, a new animal. We are dragon parents: fierce and loyal and loving as hell. Our experiences have taught us how to parent for the here and now, for the sake of parenting, for the humanity implicit in the act itself, though this runs counter to traditional wisdom and advice.*"

19

THE VISIONARY

When I emailed Yuval Noah Harari, author of two of the most important books I've ever read, *Sapiens* and *Homo Deus*, to ask if I could interview him for my book, I never thought I would get a response, let alone an affirmative one. So, when his assistant emailed me to say that he would be happy to answer my interview question upon his return from a meditation in India, my jaw dropped.

Harari is an Israeli historian and a professor at the Hebrew University of Jerusalem. The books I mentioned above are international bestsellers, touted by both Barack Obama and Bill Gates. I read *Sapiens* while in Uganda last year and walked away with a clear sense that there are two very different worlds: the world as it is, and the world as we understand it. He is an extraordinary storyteller with the ability to take complex information and make it not only comprehensible but entertaining and thought-provoking. For example, have you ever considered why we Americans so love our lawns? The excerpt below, from *Sapiens*, explains the origin of these vast expanses of green.

"Well kept lawns demanded land and a lot of work, particularly in the days before lawnmowers and automatic water sprinklers. In exchange, they produce nothing of value. You can't even graze animals on them, because they would eat and trample the grass. Poor peasants could not afford wasting precious land or time on lawns. The neat turf at the entrance to chateaux was accordingly a status symbol nobody could fake. It boldly proclaimed to every passerby: 'I am so rich and powerful, and I have so many acres and serfs, that I can afford this green extravaganza.' The bigger and neater the lawn, the more powerful the dynasty. If you came to visit a duke and saw that his lawn was in bad shape, you knew he was in trouble."

As a result, we have come to associate these worthless plots of land with wealth and power. Except in cities, nice front lawns are one of the most coveted features of a new home.

This is not a criticism; Harari is not condemning you for your desire to have a lawn. Rather, it's a question of awareness. Have you before considered why you might want a lawn? Probably not. The same can be said for many of the decisions—both large and small—that we make every day of our lives. Once you start thinking about these things, questioning why you do the things you do, you can begin to exercise more control over your own life. Further, just as I encourage everyone to interact with people from diverse backgrounds, cultures, races, and religions, I believe it is important to "interact" with history. We can learn as much, if not more, from traveling back in time as to Morocco, Peru, or New York City.

"This is the best reason to learn history: not in order to predict the future, but to free yourself of the past and imagine alternative destinies." ~ Yuval Noah Harari

In his second book, *Homo Deus*, Harari focuses on the future as it pertains to technology and, specifically, artificial intelligence. He discusses its social, economic, and political impact. Harari's hypotheses about A.I. are both fascinating and terrifying.

As I'm the mother of three teen and preteen kids, the technology conversation currently dominating my life, however, is the one about smart phones and social media.

I am inundated daily with requests to get a cell phone, iPod, or Instagram. About two years ago, I got an iPhone for my oldest, who is now sixteen.

This was at least a full year or two after all her friends had gotten one, and I heard about it constantly. In my defense, I didn't "cave" under pressure; for weeks I was texting my daughter's friends to confirm *her* after-school or sports plans, no doubt annoying the piss out of them. I finally decided she needed her own cell phone. But social media was still a definite no. The "social media ban" was not because I didn't trust her (she is more cautious and responsible than I have ever been), but because I knew—and know—firsthand how addictive social media can be, and how detrimental it *must* be to the growing brains of these young kids. As a young person, I did just about every drug imaginable; social media scares me more.

In fact, about a year ago, my oldest admitted that she was ever-so-slightly happy about not having social media; she saw her friends becoming withdrawn, some even seeming depressed, and she thought the two might be connected. As time passed, however, social media quickly became her peers' main line of communication.

I started to be unsure of whether a "total ban" was in my daughter's best interest. In fact, a friend warned me that she might become the "Catholic schoolgirl of social media," leaving home at eighteen and going social media crazy. Because Yuval Noah

Harari has an astoundingly firm grasp of history and has made some of the most compelling appraisals of the future that I've encountered to date, I thought it prudent to ask him for his opinion on the matter. After I received his response, my friend's warnings made more sense to me. I still believe that postponing social media until well into the teen years is important, but I decided to lift the ban for my oldest. She now has Instagram.

We have been working on a system that—I hope—is teaching her how to control social media rather than allowing it to control her. Thus far, we've been successful. If you are interested in ways to help your kids develop healthy social media habits, connect with me at amycarst.com.

THE INTERVIEW
(Yuval Noah Harari)

Like all technology, social media is neither good, nor bad, nor neutral. It can change the world for better or for worse—and it cannot be ignored. I think banning kids from using social media altogether is a dangerous gambit, because they live in a world where social media is an extremely important medium. It might be difficult for them to understand the world if they are totally unfamiliar with social media.

On the other hand, I agree that social media should be handled carefully. What is happening today with social media is really a global experiment on billions of guinea pigs. We have no idea what the impact might be on society and on individual minds.

The crucial thing is to use technology towards your aims, but don't allow technology to use you or to dictate your aims. Take your smartphone, for example. Does it serve you, or do you serve it? In order to answer this question, you first need to find out who you are and what your aims are in life. This is, of course, the oldest advice in the book: know thyself. But this advice was never more urgent than in the twenty-first century. Because now you have competition. Google, Facebook, Amazon, and the government are all relying on Big Data and machine learning to get to know you better and better. Once they know you better than you know yourself, they can control and manipulate you. If you want to stay in the game, you have to run faster than Google and Facebook.

So how do you get to know yourself better? I wouldn't recommend total disconnection from social media, but I would recommend that every person disconnect from the technological network for at least a few hours every week, and just come to know the immediate reality of your own mind and body. I personally dedicate two hours every day to meditation, and every year take a long meditation retreat of between thirty and sixty days. I practice Vipassana meditation, which I have learned from a teacher called S. N. Goenka (www.dhamma.org). Vipassana is a method for observing the mind in a systematic and objective manner.

The mind is constantly in contact with bodily sensations. In every moment, we are experiencing some sensation within the body, and the mind reacts to it. Even when we think that we are reacting to an email, or a tweet, or a YouTube video, we are in fact reacting to some bodily sensation. In Vipassana one trains oneself to observe, in an orderly and objective way, the body's sensations and the mind's reactions to them, thereby uncovering our deepest mental patterns. Thus, meditation is not an escape from reality. It is getting in touch with reality.

The bottom line: for at least two hours each day I actually observe reality as it is, while for the other twenty-two hours I get overwhelmed by emails and tweets and funny cat videos.

20

RESIST

Throughout human history, anger has been a part of every revolution. And it's an essential component to any revolution's success. My friend Siobhan is angry. More specifically, she's angry at classism in America. This wasn't a concept I fully comprehended before meeting Siobhan. I mean, if someone had asked me four or five years ago whether I thought classism was a problem in this country, I'm sure I would have said yes. But I don't think I would have understood, nor would I have contemplated, *why* it is a problem.

The debate about class structure in American society is not, however, what drew me to Siobhan, an English woman who spent half of her childhood in the U.K. and the other half in a hippy commune in Vermont. She has a quality about her, unlike anything I have witnessed in another human to date. She seems to transcend all aspects of not only class structure but also the more accepted divisions based on age, ability, and cognitive function. Go to a party at Siobhan's, and you're just as likely to meet bikers and black people as adults with autism and Oxford professors. Siobhan considers several children—between the ages of four and sixteen—to be some of her best friends, and she similarly regards just as many octogenarians.

Whether you're young or old, fat or thin, rich or homeless, if you are nice to Siobhan, you are her friend. What a different world we would live in if everyone chose friends based, quite simply, on how they were treated by them. As I've said at other points in this book, tolerance for different lifestyles, races, religions, and abilities should not be reserved solely for people who belong to current "hot button" categories, a.k.a. Muslim, black, or gay. Tolerance and respect should be shown towards *all* humans equally—"hillbillies," children, and the elderly included. All humans should be treated with love, kindness, and dignity. Don't allow society to dictate to whom you should show respect. Be kind. Be compassionate.

Resist.

THE INTERVIEW
(Siobhan)

Class is at the root of the structure of American society, and class is what's wrong—in my opinion—*with* American society. What makes America different from the rest of the world is that, here, we have no language for class. Without language to describe a *working* class, there can be no language for class pride.

What the rest of the world calls 'working class,' America calls 'poor.'

Everyone working two jobs to support kids they never get time to play with understands the great American lie—that if you try anything in this land of opportunity you can succeed. In a country with strikingly low social mobility, people with privilege, wealth, education, and health care are lucky. Yet they don't see their good fortune as a stroke of luck; much of the American middle class treats poor people with contempt, believing themselves to be somehow superior (intellectually, culturally) and therefore deserving of what they have. I despise this aspect of modern American culture. I have been their waitress, their kids' teacher, their cleaner, their library story-hour colleague, and I have an anger rising in me that cannot be extinguished.

What makes me not buy into any of this with my

friendship? With my heart? With my life? This is what resistance looks like. You resist by not accepting these divisions. If class is the wall that divides America, then race, gender, religion, and sexual orientation can be seen as the pictures on the wall.

And it doesn't stop there. Old people have fewer choices; children are rarely afforded real interest; and fat and stupid remain 'accepted' prejudices.

I love people, always have, it's my driving interest. I grew up in a revolutionary socialist household; I've done every shitty job on earth. I've been wealthy; I've been broke; I've been to one of the 'best' universities in the world. My usual litmus test of a person is: *are they nice to me?*. Alone I can't change the world, but I also will not be oppressed in this way. I am me. You are you.

Nice to meet you.

21

THE REFUGEE

I've tried and failed at many things and will continue to do so throughout my life. Fortunately, my fear of failure disappeared a long time ago. I love new ventures, whether or not they are successful, because I learn so much from them.

A few years back, I discovered that in the state of Vermont you can become a lawyer without going to law school. A process known as "reading the law" allows you to apprentice under a lawyer for four years, sit for the bar exam and—if you pass—become a lawyer! Reading the law, which only remains in a handful of states, is actually how Abraham Lincoln became a lawyer.

There are many differences between Mr. Lincoln and me; one of them is that he finished his law studies, whereas I made it through about four months. Despite realizing early in the process that I never want to be a lawyer, I got a lot out of those four months...and I met Bor!

I was apprenticing under an attorney at the Vermont Human Rights Commission (HRC), where Bor works as an administrative law examiner. An attorney herself, Bor has chosen meaningful work with a much lower salary than she could get working in a different field. But that's not what I found so interesting about her.

Sitting in HRC meetings, I learned quite a bit, namely that discriminatory practices are much more prevalent in my beloved—and purportedly progressive—state of Vermont than I had ever imagined. I also learned that, whether the discrimination is based on gender, race, sexual orientation, religion, national origin, or disability, there are some very impressive people fighting for our rights.

Bor is one of those impressive people.

But mostly, there is just something special about Bor. She knows the *right* thing to say, even when it's not the *easy* thing to say; she commands respect. I've heard some tough questions asked of Bor—the kind that make you cringe and think, *Thank God I don't have to answer that.* She always responds with ease and grace. Bor is witty and sharp, but not in a condescending way. She doesn't make you feel incompetent or small; she makes you feel important. There is a very appealing authenticity to Bor. I immediately wanted to be her friend. I also knew that Bor had come to the U.S. from Laos as a refugee. Although she was a very young child at the time, her journey from Laos to Chicago then to the Midwest, and eventually to Vermont, has been largely influenced by the struggles she and her parents and siblings faced nearly four decades ago.

THE INTERVIEW
(Bor)

I am sitting in front of the Mekong River at sunset, my body at ease and at home with the music, and familiar but foreign voices around me. The night market is setting up behind me, and locals and tourists begin to crowd under colorful tents. The river is wide but low and dry this time of year, and I can easily see patches of tall green grass separating Laos from Thailand. The sun is setting behind undefined clouds, creating a warm and soft light. The chance to sit down and feel the breeze from the river is respite after walking all day in the heat. The last time I was in front of this river was before I could form any memories, almost forty years ago.

The secret war in Laos had come to an abrupt end. After using men like my father, grandfather, and uncle to fight the front lines of a clandestine war—orchestrated entirely by the CIA—we were deserted without notice, provisions, or any means of escape. When my uncle returned to his troops with news that the Americans had left the country, he and his troops were faced with two options: stay and continue to fight a losing war or take their families across the jungles of Laos, by foot, to Thailand. Surrendering to the enemy was not a viable option. The idea that men who had just spent years in warfare could just walk out of the jungle, place their weapons at their feet, waive their "white flags," and re-enter society peacefully was not realistic. Some families stayed in the jungles of Laos and remain there today, forty years later. Once soldiers for the CIA, they are now considered terrorists.

I was less than two years old when my family decided we would escape to Thailand. My right leg was left paralyzed by the polio virus the previous year and—because I was no longer able to walk—my mother carried me on her back. My father carried supplies and rice, and supervised my older sister, seven, who walked on her own. My other sister, five at the time, was accompanied by my grandparents and two aunts, who were not much older than my sisters. My uncle, his wife, and their children were with us, as well as several other families from my father's troop. Traveling in a large group allowed the families to share supplies, provide support and information...but underneath this sense of safety was a crippling fear of discovery and death. Parents were pressured to give their infants opium to sedate them. Knowing that I was a quiet infant, my parents lied daily to their group, telling the others that I had taken the substance. When some of these babies died from an overdose, parents mourned their greatest loss and failures in complete silence.

Food was scarce and strictly rationed until we were close to a village and members could descend and get supplies. There were times where we resorted to eating what was around us, including tree bark and unfamiliar vegetation. My father once said, "When you feel the deep aching pain of a stomach that has been empty for days, watching your children suffer the same, you remember the privilege of having food seasoned by salt, and your head makes unthinkable and impossible bargains."

Years later, my mother and I cried together when she shared the story of a couple they met at a resting point. An injured man was waiting to reunite with his wife, two small children, and a young brother, who were traveling alone. Lost and needing to move faster, the wife left her two children with her brother-in-law, while she went in search of her husband. Upon reaching her husband, she was shocked to find that the brother-in-law had left the children alone and followed her. Still injured and exhausted, husband and wife rushed back to where she had left the children, tracing her steps. They found them exactly where she had left them. Both had died, their little bodies still warm to the touch.

When our group neared the Mekong River, they strategized how they would cross the following night. Being a mountainous people, no one knew how to swim. Using plastic as makeshift floatation devices, they taught each other to stay afloat, but there was no certainty and there would only be one trial. It was a sleepless night, being so close to the river and hearing continuous gunshots. The river was heavily guarded by Pathet Lao soldiers who were shooting anyone crossing it.

The Mekong raged the night my mother and I crossed it in complete darkness. The darkness occasionally lit up by the rapid fire of gunshots; blades of grass propelled in a frightening motion before and behind us. At the river, my mother watched the current carry people away until they disappeared. It was chaos, with hundreds of families crossing at the same time. Faces and bodies no more than shadows—everyone a stranger, indistinguishable. She called up to a God she didn't know existed. Then she blew air into the plastic bags, tied them up, and put them under her arms. With me on her back, she looked ahead, determined to kick her legs until they failed her, or she felt solid ground beneath her.

My father and oldest sister made it across, but we were separated for several days. My grandparents, aunts, and five-year-old sister had been captured by soldiers and detained. Later, my father asked for money from my maternal uncle who had been in America for a few months. When we received that money, my father used it to bribe Laotian soldiers to release my grandparents, aunts, and sister. We were reunited at the refugee camp, our home for a few months until we were sponsored by an agency in Chicago.

In the Midwest, there was a lot of support from American families and agencies, and in general. We felt welcomed but adjusting was difficult. When cars backfired, it took time for their minds and bodies to not react to gunshots and bombs. They slept on the hard floors until they got used to mattresses. In Laos, we lived in villages with extended families; here we were separated from them by hundreds of miles. (The United States tries to spread out refugees across the country so as not to burden any one location.)

We lived in Chicago's poorest neighborhood. Prostitutes loitered the street in front of our high-rise. One time, a pervert revealed himself to my oldest sister in an elevator; my father ran through the halls of the apartment with a rifle, with no concept of law and order. Another time, my father was beaten and robbed by a group of gang members at a park. We finally left Chicago for Wisconsin, and then Minnesota, to be closer to family.

One of my only pictures from my childhood is of my father holding me, next to my two sisters. In the background is an old stained mattress and window sills with crackled and scaled patterned paint, signs of lead. When welfare was insufficient to support a large family, my parents went to work as laborers and machine operators while we went to public school. There, we were told by teachers to abandon our native tongues for the more sophisticated and less primitive English. Every fall before school started, our family went to K-mart to buy new clothes. We each picked out two long-sleeve shirts and two pairs of pants, as those were items that could be worn all year. All seven of us split one packet of pens and pencils, and within a week, I had lost mine. At home, we took turn sharing pencils to do our homework. Before asking my parents if I could have money for candy or trinkets, I'd look inside their wallets to gauge how much I could reasonably request. Often, I'd find their wallets and purses empty, and so I did without too. In these moments, I wondered if my parents ever regretted crossing the Mekong. I know what they would have said if asked, "There's no time and point in regret."

As the horizon fades into a dark hue at the Mekong River, I remember the people that remained in the jungles of Laos. I think about the infants that died from opium, the story of the couple that lost their two children in the jungle, and the men, women, and children who remain at the bottom of this river. My thoughts drift to those that surrendered, survived, and wished they had crossed this river forty years ago.

Mostly, I am in awe of my parents.

I imagine the me who would have been raised in Laos compared to the me that made it through that jungle, across that river, and to America. I feel grateful.

I stand up and join the market, as both a local and a tourist.

22

THE PASTOR

As an atheist, I have always had somewhat of an aversion to organized religion. Unlike many atheists, however, I am not entirely convinced that "this is all there is." That being said, my ideas about the unknown have more of a scientific basis than a religious one. But I am an open-minded, curious individual, with the good fortune to have met several religious people in recent years who have improved—for lack of a better word—my perspective on religion, and Christianity in particular.

Susan McKnight was the beloved pastor at the Warren United Church in Vermont's Mad River Valley (my local community) for years until she retired last year. Immediately following her retirement, she and her husband Michael decided to come to Uganda to visit the Malayaka House orphanage and go on a Malayaka House Safari (a business we started to generate income for the orphanage and provide vocational training opportunities for the kids as they grow into young adults). Since then, I've gotten to know Susan quite well. And I like her...a *lot*.

I approached Susan about being interviewed for the book because she is compassionate and giving, open-minded and forward-thinking, and entirely without judgment for those she helps. This isn't always the case with deeply religious people.

I can honestly say that no piece of writing has ever had such a positive impact on my view of religion. Susan's words brought tears to my eyes, and she has dramatically influenced my ideas about religion, something for which I've held actual disdain for much of my life.

While I'm not converting to Christianity, Susan has given me a new perspective; that's a powerful, beautiful thing. She focuses on Jesus' emphasis on compassion, freedom from self, forgiveness, and tolerance, rather than the idea of deity. Reading her words, I've come to see that following the word of Jesus can be very much like following the teachings of Buddha.

And that's something I can get down with.

THE INTERVIEW
(Susan)

I often urge people not to give up on Jesus because of the imperfect, troubling attitudes and actions of many of his so-called followers. I almost did. Growing up as a P.K. (preacher's kid), I was both witness to and recipient of some of those imperfections and, when I went to college, I ran away from both God and the church. About seventeen years later, I found myself at the bottom of life (a suicide attempt), where I encountered God in a new way, specifically through Jesus, whom I believe to be the best and truest representation of God we yet have. This encounter, and the relationship that developed from it, has changed my life. Here are the gifts that Jesus has offered me—some of the reasons I not only committed myself to his movement but even became a pastor.

Healing. As I read the gospel accounts of Jesus' life, a new realization stood out: the man was always in the MIDST of healing someone dis-eased in body, mind or spirit, or coming FROM such a healing, or on his way TO a healing which someone—usually a desperate family member of the afflicted—had requested. These healings seemed to parallel my own, bringing not only miraculous relief from physical/emotional pain and shame, but providing a new sense of wholeness in myself, and a healthier connection with others.

Forgiveness. Most of the major religions have many good and important things in common, but Jesus' emphasis on forgiveness is unique to Christianity. I appreciate this emphasis—both God's forgiveness of us, and our need to forgive each other—because forgiveness is a game changer for those of us who count ourselves as members of the human race. It is what makes it possible for us to break the chains of past hurts, to re-establish human ties when they are so inevitably and regularly broken by our flawed ways of being with one another, and to prevent the spiraling of resentment and violence that can threaten the very existence of our species.

An alternative to fear. Jesus' words about fear are in keeping with the general and frequent message proclaimed throughout biblical history by prophets and angels. That message is this: "Do not fear, Be not afraid." I don't believe the admonition insinuates that we should not FEEL fear; after all, it is a natural human emotion designed to help us be safe. Instead, since fear can bring out our worst character defects and thwart us from doing the right thing when it feels too scary, we are urged not to let fear take root and get the best of us, preventing us from living

God's best life for us. As someone once said, when it comes to doing something we know to be good and right, but we hesitate due to the riskiness of that action, we should "feel the fear and do it anyway." I find the best antidote to fear is faith—faith that God is with me and will equip me to face whatever comes and accomplish whatever needs doing—especially when the result will be a better way of living/being for myself and others.

Freedom from Self. Self-centeredness is an inborn quality that helps ensure our survival as individuals, individuals who enter this world in an extremely helpless and vulnerable state. While this quality has its benefits early on in our lives, it also holds inherent dangers if left unchecked and unchanged as we develop. It can lead to great unhappiness and isolation in a person, and great conflict and unrest in communities and societies. We must counteract this need to focus on ourselves, to be unique as individuals; this is another need—to be interdependent with others. In fact, interdependence is an important part of our hard-wiring as well, and necessary for our survival as a species. If we want to thrive, both as individuals and as societies, each of us needs to grow and mature, and transition from a "community for me" mentality to a "me for community" construct. Jesus taught this truth with both his words *and* his life. He made it clear that the greatest person is not the one who has power and wealth, but instead, the one who serves others. "Love your neighbor as yourself" assumes that we start with a healthy love of ourselves and use that as a springboard and a basis to love others. (Seems to me that many people today have a hard time loving their neighbors because they don't have a healthy love for themselves!) He even goes so far as to instruct us to love those who are different from us and those we consider our enemies. This love is not a mushy feeling, but a decision—a decision to treat the other person with the respect and dignity due them as the fellow child of God they are.

Compassion. This is related to our need to connect and care, to live interdependently, as described above. It is the ability and willingness to "feel with" another person—to see that person's suffering and to take action to relieve the suffering. It is a quality we grow into, *if* we have good guidance...and all the major religions offer such guidance. Jesus was exceptional in the way he lived and offered compassion. We've already seen evidence of that compassion in the many ways he relieved people's suffering through healing. Some of the diseases he removed from people—leprosy, for example—had been not only painful physical burdens, but social ones as well. Those infected were set apart in colonies outside towns and cities and, when they ventured onto nearby roads for any purpose, were forced to shout "Unclean! Unclean!" and move to the side of the road to warn and protect other travelers who might be approaching. Hence, when Jesus touched and healed people of this dreaded disease, he also healed them of their lonely and shameful status as outcasts.

It is instructive to see how Jesus also related to others who were on the fringes of society. His acceptance of women as equals was radical in his time, as was his kind treatment of Samaritans, considered half-breeds in his Jewish culture. He took time out of his busy schedule to bless children. He invited tax collectors (and other "sinners") into his company and his community of followers; people of this profession were hated by his peers, as they were seen as collaborators of the Roman Empire in occupied Israel. He had a special heart for the mentally ill ("demon-possessed" in biblical terms) and the poor. In fact, he made it clear that the way we treat "the least of these" is the way we treat him [Matthew 25:40]. In other words, Jesus welcomed and accepted people nobody else wanted to be around—and he was criticized for it by the religious and societal bigwigs.

An important component of this compassion is refraining from judging others [Luke 6:37]. Jesus makes it clear that instead of finding fault with others, we are to use that energy to examine our own heart, motives, and actions, and clean those up. That should keep us plenty busy.

Dedication to Justice. This is a natural outgrowth of compassion. It is the motivation to right the wrongs of society which lead to someone's suffering. It is an effort to live out the Lord's Prayer which Jesus taught—specifically the lines, "Thy kingdom come. Thy will be done, on Earth as it is in heaven."

It is important not to ignore or minimize the damage that has been done in the name of Christianity. A number of horrible practices and actions have been foisted on the world and its inhabitants by so-called followers of Christ. It is ALSO important not to ignore or minimize the GOOD things that have been wrought by the Church over the ages. In this country alone, schools, colleges, and hospitals were built by churches. The Abolitionist and—later—the Civil Rights movements were started and fueled by faith-filled people. There are many people of faith active today in prison justice, natural disaster relief, human-trafficking cessation, gun-law reform, gay rights, and environmental action, and a number of churches are offering sanctuary to immigrants subject to unjust deportation.

The ways and teachings of Jesus were intensely countercultural in his time and place and have been so ever since. It takes courage to follow in his footsteps and—as has been mentioned—sometimes his followers have lost their way and their will, choosing instead to take the easier course, stepping into the prevailing principles and practices of the society around them.

But even in times when some Christians get co-opted by the culture, there are always others who courageously adhere to the ways of Jesus, sometimes in a costly way. In Germany in the nineteen-thirties and -forties, many Christians were complicit with Nazi policies and atrocities. I weep—WEEP— to think of it. And yet, there were others like pastor and theologian Dietrich Bonhoeffer, who protested the evils of nationalism, white supremacy and genocide—and paid with his life.

There are parallels in our own setting today. There are numerous white evangelicals who, for reasons beyond my comprehension, have aligned themselves with a president whose character and behavior and policies are the antithesis of Jesus. (Again, I weep.) And yet—and YET—there are many other Christ-followers who are boldly, vehemently but non-violently speaking truth to power and confronting the mean-spirited, oppressive and dangerous policies of those currently in authority. Rev. Jim Wallis of the Sojourner movement was arrested in the U.S. Capitol rotunda during discussions about the recently enacted tax "reform" plan, as he and other pastors read the 2,000 scripture passages pertaining to how we should treat the poor. Rev. William Barber II is the head of The Poor People's Campaign, which, as its website explains, is "uniting tens of thousands to challenge the evils of systemic racism, poverty, the war economy, ecological devastation & the nation's distorted morality." I've been in three marches in the past year and have seen many of my church friends there, and I know they're signing untold numbers of petitions, as am I.

It is important not to paint all Christians with the same brush.

Joy. Despite what some may believe, the Christian faith isn't just about what happens after we die; it's about the life we're living right now. Jesus said he came that we may have life and have it abundantly—to the full. [John 10:10] He also said, "These things I have spoken to you, that my joy may be in you, and that your joy may be full." [John 15:11] Joy, to me, is distinct from happiness. Happiness is generally connected to outer circumstances. Things are going well, we're getting our way, there's a pint of Ben & Jerry's in the freezer—we're happy. Joy is different. Joy is an inside job and can exist even in the midst of difficult circumstances. It is not dependent on what's happening around us but instead on the faith that whatever is going on, God is with us (we are never alone!) and can bring something good from the challenges at hand.

In addition, if we do the things that Jesus taught and encouraged us to do, the result is joy. Science agrees. Studies have shown that the people who report to be the happiest/most joyful are those who live with compassion, humility [knowing ourselves as "right-sized"—not better, not worse, than others], generosity, and forgiveness—who see themselves not as rugged individualists but as part of something bigger than themselves. Clearly, this position is also countercultural in a society that worships materialism, values personal freedom over the common good, and believes that getting and having stuff (the more, the better), and dominance over others, are the keys to having a good life.

Yes, I have received some amazing gifts in and through my connection with Jesus. As a result, my outlook on life has been transformed. In the past, there was an NPR show entitled "This I Believe."

From where I stand now, these would be my "This I Believe" statements:

I believe that each and every one of us is created by God—in love and with a special purpose.

I believe that it's never too late for someone to change. No one is outside God's possibility of hope.

I believe that there's much more to our reality than can be seen with our physical senses or through scientific knowledge.

I believe that we are blessed to be a blessing.

I believe that this world is a beautiful gift to us, and that it's our privilege and duty to care for it in the best and most intentional way possible.

I believe the words of Psalm 30:5, which assure us that while weeping may endure for the night, joy comes in the morning.

I believe that practicing gratitude and forgiveness can transform both us and the world around us. If more of us did just those two things, life would be very different on many levels.

I believe that the hardest things that happen to us can actually be the greatest gifts. I saw a great quote once by Mary Oliver:

"Someone I loved once gave me a box full of darkness. It took me years to understand that this too, was a gift."

Those words have certainly been true in my own

life. The things that I thought were going to take me out—sexual abuse, depression, suicide attempt, divorce, widowhood, among other things—have been the events that God has used to make me both stronger and more compassionate toward others in the same situations. Those difficulties opened up new compassion compartments in me that didn't exist before—or weren't very developed. They're the places where I now experience the strongest connections with others.

I believe there's much truth in the words of G.K Chesterton:

"Christianity has not been tried and found wanting; it has been found difficult and not tried."

I am grateful beyond words for the gift and opportunity to live and walk in the way of Jesus who came to make manifest both the hospitality and the new community of God. While I do so VERY imperfectly and sometimes feebly, it has made all the difference in my life. I recognize this faith walk as a lifelong process. I can say, along with TV preacher Joyce Meyer:

"I may not yet be where I WANT to be in my faith walk, but I'm surely not where I USED to be! And I give thanks."

23

THE GILDED
CAGE

I can hold my own among the ultrawealthy, but I'm
rarely comfortable. Theirs is a world so different
from mine, but in their presence, I find myself acting
like we come from the same place. Consequently,
I end up feeling like an imposter and internally
blaming them for it.

As I stand among the beautiful people—my
posture as straight and solid as a marble statue,
cocktail in hand, chin out and lips pursed in an effort
to show both curiosity and intelligence—I find
myself thinking things like, *if they walked outside and
looked in my messy car right now, they'd know I wasn't one
of them.*

But just as judging someone based on race,
religion, or low socioeconomic status is both wrong

and self-limiting, so is the assumption that the rich only want to interact with the rich. When I'm hanging out with black people, I don't pretend to be black. And I'm certain if I did, it wouldn't go over well. So, why do we feel a need to act even more privileged than we already are around the most privileged among us?

In addition to being uncomfortable and self-limiting, such behavior is actually unkind. When I think back to all of the strategic, contrived conversations I've had with ultrawealthy people to prove myself worthy of their attention, I realize how much I am likely responsible for the "lack of real connection" with people who happen to be rich, rather than the other way around. Instead of showing my authentic self, I've been presenting some pseudo-elite version of me.

But sometimes life surprises us.

About two years ago, I met Lucinda at a fundraiser for the Malayaka House orphanage. Her husband is the family friend of a longtime supporter of the orphanage, and they offered to host an event at their New York home.

Their house is stunning—a lavish estate built in the 1700s, complete with a library, hiking trails, a separate building housing a gym and sauna, an artesian well, and a sleek, gray Weimaraner named

Elsa who patrols the vast property with quiet elegance. When I pulled up to this stately house on my first visit, I immediately judged the people within it.

Fortunately, the owners of that house seemed less interested in prejudging their invited guest. Both John and Lucinda instantly struck me as down to earth, even humble. At this point, however, I assumed their modesty and unpretentiousness to be just an act, a way to relate to the commoner in their presence. But as the night progressed, their authenticity seemed more and more...authentic.

Instead of mingling and making connections with potential donors, I spent most of the evening talking to Lucinda. The conversation flowed naturally; she asked lots of meaningful questions about my life and shared equally meaningful stories of her own. We talked about a book that I was reading, *Sapiens*. Lucinda wrote down the name and said she would order it the next day. I knew that I had made a friend.

When I asked Lucinda if she would consider being interviewed for my book, I'll admit I was afraid she might find the request offensive. Nobody wants to be judged, whether for the color of their skin, their sexuality, their disability, or their wealth. I didn't want Lucinda to think that, despite our friendship, I had still placed a label on who she is as a human being.

She wasn't offended. In fact, she was more concerned about offending those less privileged by discussing the challenges of living a life of extreme privilege.

Lucinda's interview is a powerful reminder that we all struggle, no matter our race, our fame, or our wealth. Nobody gets through this life without scars. Wealth can hide suffering, but it cannot fix it. As a result, the most privileged among us often suffer in silence. This can be particularly challenging when it comes to raising kids, as Lucinda discusses in detail in her interview.

From a Buddhist perspective, extreme wealth and the possessions that go with it can easily become a source of attachment, creating a pervasive fear of loss and a constant craving. This is not to say, however, that Buddhism regards wealth negatively. In fact, traditional Buddhism actually links an individual's current wealth, at least partially, to charitable acts in a past life. Buddhism encourages privileged people to use their position for the greater good of society. The reality is, we are all capable of compassion, and we can all benefit from its healing properties. Whether we are rich, poor, or anything in between, when we show compassion to others, we heal ourselves.

"The root of suffering is attachment." ~ Buddha

THE INTERVIEW
(Lucinda)

When I was at university, I was invited by a friend to join her family at their home in the South of France. One night after dinner, we found ourselves invited to board a big, white, gleaming private yacht moored in St, Tropez harbor, alongside countless other big white yachts. It was another world, and for a while that evening we rubbed shoulders with the rich and beautiful. I'm fairly sure that, given the glamor and allure of the experience, I felt gauche and unsophisticated, somewhat out of place. But it was a seductive taste of something different, exotic, and compelling, something that shimmered, worthy of aspiration.

After the holiday, I returned home, head spinning, eager to relate my experiences of that different world. My father was busy doing some decorating in my bedroom. He was in his work clothes, sander in hand, and I must have gabbed at him about France and the yachts, the people, the lifestyle. I don't remember what I said, nor will I ever know exactly what he heard, but I imagine, given his response, that it wasn't entirely reassuring. No doubt I appeared seduced by that gilded experience, and perhaps I seemed a tad disdainful of what I had come back to, because he listened in silence and finally said, very simply and quietly as he worked away on the wall, "Well, I hope it's good enough for you back home." His words were not delivered as a reprimand. They weren't cutting or sarcastic. They were supremely leveling. They did a good job of reminding me where I had come from and who I was. They probably asked me to question who I was trying to be. Perhaps, at some level, they were a warning. But it was as much the tone of his words, which carried in it all my parents had done for me while asking for nothing back. It reminds me to this day of how easy it is to be glib and dismissive about the structure and fabric of our lives when we are dazzled by material and social things that are presented by society as precious; of how hurtful—if unintentionally—we can be towards the people around us who act selflessly in our best interests within the scope of their ability.

It made me feel ashamed.

This was one of my earlier tastes of, and lessons in, privilege. Today I live in an affluent area of upstate New York. Our community is populated by wealthy people with large country homes, apartments in Manhattan, places abroad. Some of them have trust funds, others high-level and influential professional positions in prestigious organizations. They have expensive hobbies, clubs, travel, luxury brands. Their children go to the best private schools. It is an environment in which it could be very easy to have little to no understanding of life beyond the bubble, and very easy to forget more modest beginnings.

We never know what exists behind closed doors. There are many people in our community who care very much about the world. There are certainly those who care less. Lives of privilege, as much as lives of disadvantage, can be riddled with hardship, be it loneliness, isolation, selfishness, misunderstanding. And no one is immune to tragedy. In our materialistic society, 'privilege'—wealth, achievement, success, fame, popularity—wrapped up in and presented by beautiful, smiling, seemingly carefree people, is held up as something to aspire to. Like anything, it is what we make of it, and if it doesn't enable us to look at ourselves in the mirror and see something we like, that fronts a life of meaning, then it is worthless.

When I first moved to the U.S. from England, my son was five years old. He went to public elementary school in the city, and so for six years the privilege that defined our lives was fairly diluted. But we were by no means immune to the perils. One afternoon, about a year after moving to New York City, we were out looking for a new apartment. My son was nearly six, and we were in an elevator with a real estate broker who, being friendly, asked my son what he liked to do. "Tennis and swimming," he replied. "How nice," she smiled, "and where did he do that?" "At my country club," was his innocent answer. The broker's expression said it all. My cheeks flamed. Oh, the honesty of children! The incident highlighted (not for the first time) how vigilant we need to be in the face of assumption—our own, and other people's—and the multiple implications of what we expose our children to. It also raised the burning question of when and how to more seriously introduce the concept of a world rife with inequity and inequality. It's not so easy to explain the heavily nuanced subject of privilege, and the concept of tact and discretion to a five-year-old. But it must start somewhere, and it needs to be early—ideally, of course, from the very beginning, through respect, consideration, modesty.

When my son was eleven we moved upstate, and after three years at a small private school, he moved to a private 'prep' (or high) school. For the first time, he is experiencing firsthand, and in concentration, the insidious pressures of affluence. No doubt it's a combination of age and circumstance. At fourteen years old he is able to look more astutely about him and evaluate what he sees and hears. Entitlement is rife. Some of the students wear Gucci shoes. They go shopping in Manhattan on their weekend breaks. They have access to their parents' credit cards and order what they want, when they want. There seem to be few boundaries. Some of these kids have been farmed away from home, presumably for convenience. Like high schools anywhere, there's drinking, smoking, drugs, depression, self-harming, eating disorders. But what seems evident from more recent studies is that these problems are more concentrated and insidious within groups of high socioeconomic status, where children—pushed relentlessly towards an artificial, material 'success'; used to autonomy; force-fed a meaningless, non-nutritious diet via social media—are adrift. Where are the boundaries? Where's the discipline? Where is the fundamental quest for meaning?

I talked to my son. I have always talked to him. More than anything, I want him to have solid values and a strong sense of self. I want him to be able to resist the pull of the crowd, and not be a sheep. He needs to know that privilege doesn't equal superiority, that what we have can disappear, but that what is most important—who we really are—cannot be taken away from us. It is not the trappings of life that define us. Surely there can be little more terrifying than realizing that below the glittering surface is nothing of any substance. There will always be people who have far less materially, but are far, far richer in themselves, their compassion, what they do for others.

It is particularly since becoming a parent that I understand more completely my dad's response. We do what we can for our children, and we hope that they will do their best with it. We hope they can keep their feet on the ground, their sense of perspective, their humility. We hope they can stand staunch in the face of transitory temptations, weather the storms of peer pressure, resist depression, avoid the lure of drugs and alcohol, move beyond the perceived inferiority of not wearing the right brand of clothing. We hope they can develop and retain a sense of compassion and empathy, and above all, shun the pernicious entitlement that seems an ever-burgeoning blight in today's privileged societies. Wealth is only what we do with it and meaning exists only where there are worthy intentions.

The other day I watched the movie *Ladybird*. Sister Sarah Joan, the principal of the Catholic school, remarks that Ladybird writes with love about her hometown Sacramento. Ladybird replies somewhat dismissively that she guesses she pays attention. "Don't you think maybe they are the same thing? Love and attention?" the Sister replies.

Her words moved me deeply. I thought of the kids for whom the 'yes' and the credit card are a substitute for what they really need. We must show our children that we love and care about them by paying attention, setting them on as straight and true a path as possible, equipping them with the tools needed to evaluate people and situations of all kinds, however glitzy or not, wherever they are. The world has incredible things and incredible people in it. We do our children the greatest disservice if we don't open their eyes to all its possibility. Attention is something priceless that we are all able to give. And if we give it to our kids, wherever they are, they have the chance to weather almost anything, and do something deeply valuable with their lives.

24

LONGEVITY

In 2015, a friend introduced me to Olga Murray, a retired attorney who, for nearly thirty years, has dedicated her life to helping children in Nepal. In 1990, she founded the Nepal Youth Foundation, which has saved the lives of thousands of Nepali children through its schools, medical facilities, and children's homes.

Olga and the Nepal Youth Foundation have also managed to put a stop to the age-old practice of "selling daughters." For years, young girls were sold by impoverished families as indentured servants to wealthier families. As a result of the foundation's efforts, more than eleven thousand girls have been able to remain at home.

Although we never met in person, I called Olga with some fundraising questions that our mutual friend thought she could help me answer. When we first spoke, Olga was nearly ninety. She was friendly and very sharp, and her advice was invaluable in my efforts to overcome some non-profit hurdles with which I was dealing. During our conversation, she mentioned, multiple times, that she'd email me a relevant document or forward me a particular link. I have to admit, I doubted I'd receive at least some of that information. As someone who has always struggled with ADD, I am constantly forgetting to send people things I promise to send...and I'm barely forty!

But just as Olga had promised, every link and document arrived to my inbox within a day. She even shared a few helpful criticisms about the way I had been fundraising, and she managed to do it without making me feel incompetent. In addition to being sharp *and* tactful, she was still splitting her time between two homes: one in California and one in Nepal. *And*—I soon learned—she had a five-year plan! At ninety!

I knew I wanted to interview Olga for this book, but not having talked to her in more than two years, I was worried that she wouldn't still be actively involved with her work in Nepal. Well, my concerns were unfounded. Not only is she still involved with the Nepal Youth Foundation, she was *in* Nepal when

I contacted her. At nearly ninety-three years old, Olga Murray still travels back and forth to Nepal, and remains fully active in the non-profit she founded.

If you want to see Olga in action, check out her 2015 TED Talk entitled *What if You Could Live a Joyful and Vibrant Life at Any Age?* Olga believes that her work in Nepal is helping not only children there, but also her ability to live a fulfilling life well into her nineties.

In her TED Talk, she also tells of a San Francisco based organization co-founded in 2005 by her friend and age-mate Ruth Maguire, to end the United States military's presence in the Middle East. Grandmothers Against War opposes all wars, but in the early days they were particularly focused on the war in Iraq. One of their primary tactics was to stage "die-ins." They would lie down on the sidewalk, their arms outstretched and their eyes closed tight, and they would block the entrance to military buildings, such as the U.S. Army headquarters in Oakland.

One of my favorite parts of Olga's TED Talk is when she says, "I can tell you that the police were terrified of these women; the last thing they wanted to do was arrest a bunch of sweet old grandmothers who were protesting an unjust war."

Their message: Take us instead. Do not sacrifice the lives of our grandchildren in a senseless war. Ruth continued her work, giving out anti-war pamphlets in San Francisco's Union Square every Thursday, until she passed away at ninety in December of 2015.

People like Olga and Ruth are my role models. As I said earlier in this book, my career is not something from which I want to one day retire. I hope to be writing and advocating for social justice well into my nineties and beyond. Too many people retire at sixty-five and just slowly fade away. This thought causes me intense sadness. I wish that more people would follow in the footsteps of Olga Murray, those feisty grandmothers, and anyone else who realizes that to live purposefully and compassionately is to live well.

And how can you die when you always have a five-year plan??

THE INTERVIEW
(Olga)

Amy: I started out as an insurance broker and didn't find my path (human rights work and writing) until my mid-thirties. At first, I felt like I had wasted much of my life. In time, however, I realized the benefits to this "delay."

The juxtaposition of a life with purpose and a life without has helped me appreciate everything so much more. I know you started your work in Nepal later in life, after spending most of your career as an attorney in California. What were the benefits of your "delay"?

Olga: I was fortunate to have a job that I felt promoted social justice. I was an attorney with the California Supreme Court for thirty-seven years, and my job was to draft opinions for the justice I worked for. These involved many of the most important social issues of the day, and since I worked for a justice with whom I saw eye to eye on most questions of the day—civil rights, racial and gender and economic issues—I felt I was making a contribution to society during my working years. My only regret is that I did not start my work in Nepal sooner, because we could have had an even greater impact on the lives of children here.

However, I learned a good deal during my time as an attorney that helped to promote and inform my work in Nepal. I was able to use my legal knowledge to form the foundation, and I made contacts during my many working years that helped to jump start financial support for the foundation's programs. Because of my longevity, I have been involved with helping children in Nepal almost as long as I worked as a lawyer.

Amy: In my mid-thirties and with three young children at home, leaving a secure job to "follow my dream" was scary, but as soon as I embarked on that path, things began falling into place. I know lots of other people with families to support who are unfulfilled but hesitant to leave secure careers to fulfill their passion. Do you have any advice for these people?

This is a complicated question. It depends on what a person's obligations are and how onerous his or her job. I was fortunate to be doing work which was enjoyable, stimulating intellectually, and important to society. Although I could have earned more in private practice, I knew the work I was doing was more fulfilling.

Still, I yearned to work directly to help children in some capacity, and I always knew I would do so ultimately. As it turned out, I began the work in Nepal at age sixty and retired six years later to devote all my time to it. I had no financial obligations to support family. Others may not be so fortunate. I think everyone has to balance these factors and find a solution that meets their and their family's circumstances. It's never too late to start.

Amy: When we spoke on the phone a few years ago, I wouldn't have known you were nearly ninety from our conversation. I'm thrilled that nothing seems to have changed, and that you're still going back and forth to

Nepal every year! Do you think that continuing to do this kind of work has had a positive impact on your health and longevity?

Olga: Yes, I definitely think so. It is thrilling to wake up each morning knowing that I—through our foundation—will do something that day to help a child, or many children. I look forward to every day.

My work here has reinforced my optimism about humanity because of the tremendous improvements we are able to make in the lives of children. I am healthy, active, and have a good memory. I believe some of this is due to the fact that this is the happiest time of my life, but also partly due to good genes. My mother lived fruitfully and in good health until she was 98 years old and although I have a way to go (I will be 93 in June), I am grateful for the good genes she passed on to me.

25

THE ADDICT

Addiction isn't only about drugs and alcohol. With a constant stream of information at our fingertips every second of every day, information addiction is becoming increasingly prevalent. Addictions can take countless forms—drugs, money, sex, gambling, food, information, power, and any other temporarily rewarding activity with negative consequences. But society accepts certain addictions, namely, money, power, and information. As a result, those who suffer from a societally accepted addiction often do so for a lifetime.

But not so with drugs and alcohol. The suffering attached to this type of addiction generally only ends in one of two ways, sobriety or death. In my opinion, an addiction to money is no less tragic than an addiction to crack, but where "crackheads" are locked up and shamed, those addicted to money and power are revered and rewarded.

Those who manage to overcome an addiction, however, often go on to lead extraordinarily fulfilling lives. Such is the case with my new friend, Todd Giorgi, who overcame an addiction to crack and has been sober for more than seventeen years. Not only has Todd stayed true to himself, his wife Anna, and his daughter Jagger by consciously choosing sobriety every day, he lives his life to help others live *their* best lives. He is the owner and founder of NY Strong, a gym where he helps people improve their physical, mental, and emotional strength. He's a Strongman National Level Competitor, and he speaks openly about his struggle with addiction.

The world needs more openness and authenticity. In an effort to hide our flaws, we bury them so deep that even *we* have trouble digging them up and dealing with them. In essence, we hide them from our selves. And addictions are a double whammy—they are flaws we use to hide other flaws from—you guessed it—*ourselves.*

People who, like Todd, are willing to share their struggles to help others overcome theirs, are heroes. But they are also smart. Shame is much heavier when we hold it alone. If you are still holding on to shame, consider lessening that burden by opening up to someone you trust. As you will read in Todd's interview, there are always people willing to help *if* you ask.

THE INTERVIEW
(Todd)

Contrary to popular belief, marijuana isn't the gateway drug. It's alcohol. I was fourteen when I had my first drink. I was at a high school party trying to be someone I wasn't. Those feelings of not being good enough, tall enough, smart enough, or big enough enter the psyche at such a young age. That night, I was just trying to be someone people would like. The "out of control crazy kid" act worked—I was getting attention. So, I ran with it.

The very next time I drank, I blacked out. Somehow, I made it home, and my father, who was a paramedic in Harlem, came home and revived me. The next day, we spoke about being in control, and I yessed him to death. But, truth be told, I wasn't in control for a single day during the rest of the nineties.

My life consisted of getting high, drinking "40s" and smoking blunts, until I entered college. I chose UMass, mostly because it was nicknamed "the Zoo."

During my freshman year, I met a young man who introduced me to the purest flake—from Bogata, Columbia—I would ever come across. Cocaine was *it*. I felt like God. It was the greatest feeling on earth.

When you're using cocaine, you quickly recognize its power and decide it's something you'll only do every few months. For a while, that's what I did. Then I came home for winter break and introduced it to a couple of friends. Soon it had become a weekend thing. And then Saturday felt so fucking good, why not add Tuesday and Thursday? Next thing I knew, I was hooked. It got me.

My life basically revolved around cocaine—scoring it, snorting it, trying to recover from its effects. That's pretty much how it goes, until one day, you're in a car with a friend going to score, and instead of coke he buys crack. If you're looking for an express train to the bottom, this is your ticket. Crack becomes your lover, your breath, your only friend. It manipulates and humiliates. It's called the "Devil's Drug" because it takes your soul if you let it.

Crack is, without a doubt, the most addictive substance I have ever encountered. Running out of money won't stop you. Running out of gas won't stop you. Running out of work, friends, or family will not stop you. I had come from a good home with plenty of love, got decent grades, attended a well-known university, and had girlfriends galore...how did things get so out of hand?

You know how far you've fallen when you're sitting with a group of other crackheads, thinking about how to rob the local bodega, or when you stick a twenty-dollar bill through a hole in the wall of a dark alley and hope that what comes out the other side won't kill you. You know it when you steal from your family and friends. You know it when you're certain if another man told you to get down on your knees to get some crack, you would, or when you let a drug dealer in the backseat, and he puts a gun to your head and says, "You better pray you're not the mother fucking police."

I have no explanation for why I am here today, other than God's grace. I was physically, emotionally, spiritually, and financially bankrupt when I found myself at a Narcotics Anonymous meeting in a church basement. I was twenty-two years young, thankfully. Because, do you see any old crack addicts running around? Of course not...they're all dead. I knew I had to get clean, or I was going to die too.

Addiction is cunning, baffling, and powerful. And you don't need a story as hardcore as mine. You could be fooling yourself and everyone else around you, still maintaining a job, family, and friends—hiding your addiction. But through your addiction, you're also hiding from yourself. What are you hiding from? What part of your life do you not want to look at?

There are all kinds of addictions. When it comes down to it, *anything* can be a drug. My suggestion is to take a serious look at everything you're involved in and ask yourself, *Is my life better for doing this? Am I moving closer to God (or whatever you believe in)? Or is this activity, drug, or behavior moving me further away from my life's purpose?*

Today I live happy, joyous, and free. And I have four absolutes: absolutely no crack, cocaine, heroin, or alcohol. Those four things moved me away from the God that lives within me. Today, I have a clear vision of what my purpose is, so I don't venture back into that world of four. I know exactly where I'd be within a few hours.

I strive to act, speak, and do in such a way that those who come in contact with me will say their life is better for it. In this way, I can be of service. I can share the horror stories of my past, helping people—young and old—to avoid going down that same dark path. *This* is my legacy.

I'm sitting in Starbucks as I write this and *Lean On Me* is streaming. I can't help but get choked up because the song says it all. I would be dead today if not for the good of humanity. There are people out there who will do absolutely anything to help you *if* you want to be helped. I was picked up from the gates of Hell and carried until I could walk again. How could I possibly not give that back to humanity??? Why would I not be vulnerable and show the world who I am?

I know what it's like to struggle, to be on the bottom—to be shamed and *ashamed*. I should be dead, but I'm not. Living *alive* is a choice. I choose to live today in a way that helps others avoid making the same mistakes I made, and to prove that there are still good people on this earth who care for the greater good. Sober for more than seventeen years, I am living proof that "once an addict, always an addict" is a lie.

"Don't ask what the world needs. Ask what makes you come alive, and go do it. Because what the world needs is people who have come alive." ~ Howard Thurman

26

THE ARAB
WORLD

In January 2017, I traveled to Jordan to interview refugees living at al Zataari, the world's largest Syrian refugee camp, in anticipation of the proposed resettlement of one hundred refugees to the Vermont city of Rutland. I stayed at the Amman Pasha hotel in Amman, Jordan's vibrant capital. For about twenty U.S. dollars per night, I got a private room and bath, access to a rooftop deck with insane views of the city, and a delicious complimentary breakfast every morning in the downstairs cafe. My room was clean and pleasant, but I only used it to sleep and shower.

The cafe became my second home. I was traveling solo and expected the same experience in Amman as I would have had in, say, London or New York

City—polite smiles and friendly people but no real connections being made. I was completely wrong.

For starters, the Jordanian men who worked, played music at, and—presumably—lived in the hotel, were some of the most welcoming, hospitable people I've met in my life. And not in a flirty or aggressive way. They were kind, and seemed truly concerned with my happiness, comfort, and overall well-being. One morning, I came down for my "usual" breakfast—falafel, chick pea salad, hummus, a hard-boiled egg, and a cup of Arabic coffee—and Ibrahim, one of the guys who worked there, noticed I didn't look my chipper self. "Are you feeling okay this morning, madame?" I was a bit embarrassed, as my current state was due primarily to the consumption of two "big size" Petra beers the night before, and Ibrahim, like many Muslim men, does not drink alcohol. But instead of judging me, he nodded his head, disappeared for a few minutes, and returned with a small package of pain relievers from the pharmacy around the corner. "Try this and drink with lots of water. You'll feel better soon."

Upon my return from Jordan, I wrote an article for the Rutland Herald, the newspaper servicing the community within which the refugee resettlement was supposed to occur. Sadly, only the first two families ever arrived to Rutland; the rest of the resettlement got caught in the crosshairs of Trump's inauguration. Below is an excerpt from that article, originally published on February 4, 2017.

Over the next few days, the tourist glasses started to slowly slip from my eyes, thanks in large part to Richard, a lovely Jordanian man who offered to be my driver for the week. Fortunately, I accepted the offer because, honestly, I think I learned more about the Middle East, Islam and Christianity in the fifteen-or-so hours we spent in the car talking than in the previous thirty eight years of my life. Richard is Christian in a predominantly Muslim country, but he loves his country and all of its people. In fact, the positive relations between Muslims and Christians in Jordan is striking. We could learn a lot.

Throughout the next week, Richard introduced me to many of his friends, most of them Muslim. I sat in the homes of several Muslim families sharing sweet treats and cups of delicious Bedouin tea (sage, cinnamon, cardamom and mint). In every home I visited, the common desire of the families to speak to me in English was sweet, and a bit embarrassing. Here I was, an American visiting their country from a place where our fears and hatred of the Middle East are plastered across social media, and they wanted to speak to me in English? I had never wanted to speak Arabic more than in those moments, to be able to tell them, "No, no, it's OK. Let's speak your language, it's beautiful."

Terrorism isn't based in religion. No, religion is an excuse. The real cause of terrorism, and violence as a whole, is suffering. I've been saying this for years, but not because of an acute understanding of Islam or the Middle East. It's simple logic. Every violent group is built on a foundation of suffering. Think of inner-city gangs. Would teenagers be standing on street corners selling drugs or stabbing other teens as part of gang initiations if all their needs were met, and they lived in safe homes with loving families, organic food and golden retrievers named Sam? Of course not.

The suffering in parts of the Middle East, Africa, India and South America is out of control. Instead of using some of our power, resources and money to help build infrastructure, schools and hospitals, we use our power, resources and money for military defense, arms and counterterrorism. We convince our citizens that Muslims, Arabs, Africans and Mexicans will either blow us up, rape our women or steal our jobs. Through the use of propaganda, we demonize these people (who, by the way, account for the majority of the global population). Why do we do this? Well, first we have to understand who "we" actually is.

In the United States, the wealthiest people and corporations have significant control over everything from the media to the passing of legislation. If rich, white, Christian American men have significant control over the media, the government, and legislation, it stands to reason that they have significant control over us, wouldn't you say? And if their values and motivations are based in self-preservation, which is to say the self-preservation of rich, white, Christian American men, can you see why Arabs, Africans, Muslims and Mexicans (and even women) might be a threat?

In much the same way that those in power in America use media to distract us from getting "too involved" (think reality TV shows, football and fake news), those in power in many of the Arab countries have their own way of distracting citizens. Keep the people hungry. If they are too distracted by starvation and the constant need to procure food, they will not get involved in politics. But, in some places, such as Syria, that plan backfired. If your entire existence becomes about getting food to feed your family, this need replaces all others. In the words of my new friend, Richard, If you give a starving man $1,000, it is a treasure. Food forever. He will do anything for it. If you give a starving man $1,000 and a gun, he will kill his brother.

Suffering breeds violence. The underlying disease of terrorism is suffering, brought on by poverty. You can treat the underlying disease, or you can treat the symptoms. While the West continues to treat only the symptoms of this suffering through war, torture, prison and occupation, groups like ISIS are treating the underlying disease. They are smart and sophisticated. Curing the underlying *disease serves their purpose. And our hatred and fear of Muslims plays perfectly into the hands of jihadist leaders. It's the best recruiting tool they could ask for. But this isn't a one-sided game. Just as terrorist groups want us to block refugees and spew hateful rhetoric to increase their ability to recruit, those in power in the U.S. benefit from terrorism. If they fear us, ISIS recruits more fighters. If we fear them, wouldn't we recruit more fighters too?*

Even with an open mind, cultural conditioning can be quite the hurdle to overcome. On our way to Petra, late one night, Richard and I stopped at a gas station for snacks. Pringles taste the same in the Middle East, by the way. As I was about to walk out of the gas station, a pickup truck pulled in front of the glass doors, stopped somewhat abruptly, and four guys dressed in long white robes and head scarves hopped out all at once. I think my heart skipped a beat. Four men in Arab dress getting out of a truck, at night? As Americans, we only see these images in the news, when the men are equipped with machine guns, shouting "Allahu Akbar!"

These guys didn't have machine guns. I continued to move forward with confidence, albeit a touch of fear. One of the men held the door for me. Distracted by the mishmash of logic and cultural conditioning scrolling through my head, I tripped over his foot. He smiled (actually, I think it was more of a giggle) and said, "sorry, madame." I *walked back to the car filled with an overwhelming sense of shame.*

When I shared my experience with Richard, he laughed. "Yes, I understand. But it's OK to feel that way, as long as you recognize it and question it. That's how we learn." Richard is a smart man. But if a person who spends her days preaching about tolerance and love can be scared of someone — even if only for a heartbeat — simply because he looks different, what about everyone else? We have an uphill battle to climb. The national dialogue about Muslims and refugees cannot be changed overnight. It will take time, and it will take personal experiences. The resettlement in Rutland could have been an answer. Now, who knows?

On one of my last nights in Jordan, the old man who owned the hotel I was staying at learned of my trip to the refugee camp. As I sat in the hotel café having my 14th Turkish coffee of the day, he sat beside me and thanked me for coming to Jordan to give a voice to refugees. He was a refugee himself, having fled Palestine in 1948, then again in 1967. He resettled in Australia, living there for almost 40 years, until returning to the Middle East, marrying, and buying a hostel in Damascus, Syria. The place quickly became a popular spot for tourists from around the world, but when the revolution began in 2011, he had to flee yet again. "So, now I am here in Jordan. I hope I don't have to flee again before I die.... I'm an old man, you know, and I love Jordan." I said, "Jordan seems safe and tolerant. I'm sure you'll be fine here." He smiled, "yes, yes, I'm sure. But then again, we're in the ring of fire here. Who knows?"

The ring of fire. As I sat there talking to this charismatic, fascinating, full-of-life, three-time refugee, I couldn't help but think, "are we the ones holding the match?"

I've kept in contact with several of the people I met in Jordan, including a Finnish woman who volunteers in animal shelters throughout the Middle East, a lovely Italian woman named Luisa who traveled with me across much of Jordan (sadly, cancer claimed Luisa's life this winter), an American serving breakfast at the Amman Pasha in exchange for housing, and my friend Richard. Fortunately, when I asked Richard if he'd be open to an interview, he said he would "love to be the man who could change the perspective of some people who do not understand life in the Middle East." I think his wish will be fulfilled. If reading Richard's interview has a positive impact on your view of the Middle East, reach out to me at amycarst.com. I'd love to be able to show him that his words have, indeed, made a difference.

THE INTERVIEW
(Richard)

The Arab world is imagined as a place of wars and instability, but it is rich with history, culture, and compassion. Also known as the Middle East, this part of the world consists of twenty-one countries, including my home country of Jordan. We are neighbored by Palestine to the west, Iraq to the east, Saudi Arabia to the southeast, and Syria to the north. Jordan is one of the few countries that managed to protect its citizens throughout all of the region's wars.

Jordan has long housed refugees, and people fleeing oppression and difficult conditions in their home countries. When the Palestinians found themselves deserted in 1948, they came to Jordan. Then Egyptians began to arrive in search of better jobs. Most recently, came the Syrians and Iraqis.

Economically, this increase of population initially caused a shortage of resources, and the government had to find new ways to accommodate so many people. But socially, the influx of refugees and immigrants has led to great diversity. And when diversity is built on principles of acceptance, it leads to respect.

My name is Richard Hanna Masreki. I am a Jordanian citizen based in the capital of Amman. I am of Aramaic descent (we are the people who spoke the language of Jesus Christ). My father was born in Jerusalem and my mother in Bethlehem. We are Christian Palestinian refugees who came to Jordan in 1948. Since arriving here, we have never once felt like foreigners. Jordan gave us citizenship, shelter and, most importantly, Jordan gave us identity.

We came here as refugees, but we quickly became natives. The credit goes to the natives, who accepted us with open arms. In Jordan, people have a strong belief that every human has the right to live and work with pride, regardless of their religion and origin.

There are two main religions in Jordan, Christianity and Islam, with the Christians forming only about 5 percent of the population. Although we are the minority, we never feel like it. We live in harmony because the Christians are respected by the royal family and the government, but most importantly, by Muslims themselves. This respect is a result of the Quran—their holy book— which tells them to respect Jews and Christians. After all, in the end we are all sons of Abraham.

Of course, there is no denying that there exist some strict Muslims who have interpreted the Quran in a very different way. Sadly, it is those who manipulate the image of true Islam for their own benefit who are perceived as "true Muslims" in the West. But these are not true Muslims. If we are to live in global harmony, this image of Muslims and the Arab world must change.

Their book does not tell them to throw bombs. Muslim girls are not forced to wear hijab nor are they banned from education. Arab Christians and Muslims are not in constant conflict. When we Christians fast, they do not eat in our presence, and when they fast, we show the same respect. We don't ride camels and tour the desert all day. We have companies, colleges, schools, and modern cities.

I am the father of two girls and a boy. My daughters are twenty-two and eighteen, and my son is twenty-one. They all still live at home. My oldest daughter studies in the university and is completing her internship at the hospital, and my younger daughter is currently in her senior year of secondary school. She loves sports and plays the bagpipes. They both have big dreams—to travel, to succeed, to be whatever they want to be. I have always encouraged this in them. My son studies, works, and is the leader in a musical band. Like his sisters, he wants to do big things. I have always loved this about my children.

I was born in a religious Christian family, but my mother always taught us about Islam. Because of this, my love and respect for Muslims grew. She taught me that when the Athan (their prayer) plays over the mosque speakers, I shouldn't talk, and when I see someone fasting during Ramadan, I shouldn't eat in front of them.

My parents were open minded enough to send me to Lebanon to study, and that was my first adventure. In that country, during 1979 and 1980, there was a civil war between Lebanese and Palestinians. Of course, the majority of Palestinians were Muslim, but they accepted me, even though I was Christian. At the time, I felt safer living among Palestinian Muslims than Christian Lebanese; that added even more to my respect for Islam. And so, I traveled more and more, but I was always homesick. Jordan never left me.

For these reasons and more, I have always felt it my job to help Westerners to better understand the Arab world and my beloved and beautiful Jordan. Thank you for this opportunity.

27

THE BUDDHIST

I wrote about Sensei Tony in the first part of this book, how his weekly Dharma talks helped me to realize that I was living someone else's life. I recently asked him how he handles the stresses of everyday life as a Buddhist, a husband, and a father. I once read something that said, "Even a Buddhist monk would struggle to remain Zen if he had a spouse, a mortgage, a couple of kids and a 9-to-5." That is, essentially, Sensei Tony's reality. He's a Buddhist minister, yes, but he's not living in a temple atop a mountain in Japan with nothing but the calls of turtle doves to distract his mind from daily meditations. Sensei Tony lives and works in Harrisburg, PA; he's married with one son; he has a mortgage and a business.

So, how does he stay so damn Zen?

THE INTERVIEW
(Sensei Tony)

As an ordained Buddhist minister, I am often asked if I ever get frustrated or lose my cool. I jokingly affirm that I am the very definition of 'chill.' However, this question goes to the heart of why many who investigate mindfulness and meditation often become frustrated, or begin with a bang and then slowly drift backwards. The question also reveals the unfortunate assumption that being enlightened is a form of perfection. Many folks interpret the teachings of Buddha through the veil of duality (one or the other), not understanding the vision of Oneness.

In my own practice, we use what I call 'Mindfulness Models.' One of these is 'Perfection versus Wholeness/Oneness.' In this model, I help practitioners understand that they have been conditioned to constantly seek a form of perfection which does not really exist. This perfection-seeking creates two possibilities: the individual is always in pursuit of the "carrot" (some ideal), or in expectation of punishment, generally in the form of failure. This vicious cycle makes us very vulnerable to manipulation; we develop an either/or approach to problems, and change becomes the enemy.

What if, instead, we exchanged the impractical cycle above for the achievable goal of Wholeness or Oneness? If we accept the good, bad, and ugly in our lives, we can learn to integrate all of these essential components in the way of *our* choosing, the most harmonious way. This practice further allows us to transform a difficult situation—even a crisis—into an opportunity to create something new. By implementing and nurturing this new view, we break the conditioning of perfectionism, and embrace a more reality-based attitude—both/and instead of either/or.

As a husband and father, I face the same vicissitudes of life as each of you. I experience moments of anxiety, anger, and sadness. But there *are* some differences. As a Buddhist minister, I have learned to experience these emotions differently, using them as a special point of practice. A long time ago, I made the conscious decision to refuse to think, say, or do anything that knowingly contributes to my suffering or that of others. I am committed to the renunciation of suffering; if I were not, I would be doing something else. I experience every human emotion—the positive ones and the painful ones. But I've learned to use them as entry points to more awakened living. Each and every one of us has the ability to do that...but it takes lots of practice.

Buddhism was not born of a one-time, perfect enlightenment experience. Rather, it emerged from the struggle to confront the great matter of life and death, to see what is beneath all the layers of our conditioning, to understand that our perception of existential separation is flawed, and false. This sense of separateness is fed by the poisons of the mind—namely, fear and a blind drive for survival. It is to discover that Oneness is not found in power, but in weakness, not in strength but in suffering, not in separation but in Interbeing.

Buddhism was borne of the tormented and weak humanity of a lonely human being. A man who had awakened to his Oneness with all life. This Way of Oneness was not a triumph, rather, it emerged from an awakening to the True Self; not from denying our imperfect humanity but by plunging deeply into the muddy waters of our very human existence.

Those who follow the Path of Awakening are like the antibodies in an unhealthy body; they are like the spices in the Supreme Meal of life, giving it a unique flavor and feeding all who hunger; they are like warm streams flowing in the deep darkness; they are like the cracks in the walls of our self-imposed prisons, letting in the Light.

Enlightenment is not a destination. It is a realization that intentionally faces and turns the fear of failure into an opportunity for a freer, fuller and more joyful life.

28

THE MEDIUM

Audrey is my husband's cousin. We had a connection from the start because she, like me, has always been a black sheep. Also like me, Audrey realized—later in life—that although her "calling" was apparent even in childhood, she had long suppressed that calling in favor of a more traditional, or accepted, path. She became the owner of a successful hair salon, bought a big house and nice cars, and continued to "live the part" well into her late thirties.

A few years ago, Audrey found herself in a difficult situation, a crossroads. She was no longer happy doing what she had been doing for her entire adult life. Even her body was telling her that something needed to change, and soon. But through that darkness, Audrey found light—as so frequently happens in a time of crisis—and she was returned to the path she began as a child, but this time without the fear of judgment (or at least, with *less* of that fear).

In my opinion, announcing to the world that you're a medium and can convene with spirits is a ballsy thing to do. Some devoutly religious people may find the assertion downright offensive, and the nonbelievers among us are likely to be skeptical at the very least. I'm an Atheist, the most skeptical of the skeptics, but I'm also open-minded (is that an oxymoron?), and I have—enthusiastically—agreed to let Audrey do channel readings for me on multiple occasions.

I don't know how she does it, or what she is doing, but Audrey somehow manages to transcend whatever wall or block my analytical brain throws up like a shield. I have been reduced to tears more than once, but more compelling is the great sense of clarity I seem to derive from each of our sessions. Whether or not Spirit is guiding Audrey, I do not know. But I *can* say this—if she's coming up with this shit on her own, her intuition is off the charts. It's otherworldly.

And maybe that's the thing about intuition—its otherworldliness. Whether that other world is brought forward by exceptional intelligence and empathy, an altered state of consciousness, or the ability to communicate with spirits, the benefits of powerful intuition cannot be discounted. I commend Audrey for listening to her body *and* her mind and using her gift to help others to do the same.

THE INTERVIEW
(Audrey)

For years, I owned a busy high-end salon. I worked twelve-hour days with no breaks, and I prided myself in always being available for my staff and clientele. But this schedule was about to catch up with me.

Plantar fasciitis and lower back pain were beginning to interfere, and the fact that I couldn't sleep at night wasn't helping. I went to doctors, physical therapists, and chiropractors, hoping that they could help me. Surgery was the only solution they offered. If I had surgery, I could maintain this crazy work schedule, and my physique. After all, my business model was based on money and appearances.

One day, as I was looking into disability insurance options, a client recommended acupuncture. I hadn't considered this possibility—and honestly, didn't think it would be aggressive enough to return me to my former self—but I decided to give it a go.

The acupuncturist was horrified by my daily routine of standing to eat because I had no time to sit and holding my bladder all day so as not to fall behind schedule. "Your body is trying to talk to you," he cautioned, "You are not a machine."

The words of my Mandarin healer were not lost on me. I became especially receptive to—and grateful for—his holistic approach as my body *actually* began to heal itself.

Then I started having "experiences" during treatments.

"What were those lava-like blobs of colorful light I saw in the room during my treatment?"

"You just saw your energy," he nonchalantly replied, on his way out of the room.

I still had more work to do. The acupuncture was healing my body, but I had to keep it in shape. Fight time. That's when I discovered yoga. *Surely yoga will maintain my figure.* Have you seen those women on the cover of *Yoga Journal*?

But what I experienced in yoga was much more than a workout. I took a full breath. I took my attention inside myself. I again saw the "colorful lava" in my mind's eye. God began whispering in my ear. My intuition heightened.

I was being called to change my life. *I have a*

purpose and it has nothing to do with hairspray and gray coverage.

My lifestyle changed drastically over the next few years. I attended countless workshops and read every metaphysical book I could get my hands on. I studied different forms of energy work and began to share what I was learning with others. Parts of myself that I had suppressed for years began to bubble up. No longer was I ashamed of the thirteen-year-old me that was sent home from church camp for having tarot cards in her suitcase or being ridiculed because I believed in faeries.

Maybe the "sparks of light" that I've been seeing my entire life are more than just my eyes playing tricks on me, as I was told by adults.

Fast forward to today. I have fully accepted my gifts. It's like a rite of passage for us adults—to realize that something which caused us so much pain, or shame, or fear for so long is actually our greatest gift.

My Spirit guide shared with me that I had shut down my ability to connect with Spirit when I was a little girl, out of fear. No adults could help me understand or nurture this part of myself. It was scary and confusing, so I abandoned it.

But in my thirties, I finally found the support I needed in a community of other truth seekers on a similar path. I became devoted—mind, body, and soul—to doing the work I was being called to do. First, I sold my sports car and got a basic Honda. Next, I sold my salon, opened a space in the barn in my backyard, and began teaching workshops and offering reiki, crystal healing, and yoga. No longer was I willing to work more than a few hours a day. "Slow and gentle" became my new mantra.

Some friends were curious about these changes and wanted a closer look. Others were perplexed and fell away. At first this hurt my heart. But I soon came to appreciate the space they left behind as a gift.

Not everyone likes this new me. But I wish them well, knowing that they will have their own spiritual awakening in their own time, even if it is in another lifetime. As I am writing this, a friend request came from a former client who unfriended me a few years back. Ten years ago, I probably would have deleted it. Now I accept...and ask God how I may be of service to this woman.

The deeper I dig, the more I uncover. One day, Spirit starts talking directly to me—spontaneously—giving me lengthy messages for people. Not only am I given visions about their future and current path, I begin to connect with their loved ones who have passed.

The connection to those who have passed isn't new, but this level of communication is. Whereas in the past, I might have smelled tobacco while working on a client and known that their grandfather was hanging around, I now feel a deeper connection to Spirit, having actual conversations with people who have left their physical bodies—people I have never met.

Friends bring friends who are strangers to me. I give them messages from their loved ones, angels, and Spirit guides. At times, I am guided to lay hands on them for channeled healing. I scan their bodies and share with them—with surprising accuracy—what ailments they have and what ailments their deceased loved ones had. Sometimes Spirit shares so much information that the person walks away with a renewed sense of their life's purpose.

These messages are healing, and not just on an energetic level. Emotional healing is evident. I see the fear of death lessen in people who have received messages from Spirit. Grief around a loved one's passing shifts. There is a new awareness.

I recently read for a long-time salon client/friend who lost her daughter in a horrific accident twenty-five years ago. The daughter gave me beautiful messages to share with her mother, showing me what she looked like the last time her mother saw her, what she was wearing, the style of her hair, things they talked about. What Spirit did not tell me was that the mother would have a stroke and leave her physical body a few weeks later. I was devastated to lose my friend in her physical form but quickly connected to her in Spirit. I am a little sad for me but *so* happy that she has finally reconnected with her daughter.

At times, even today, this path has brought me fear, heartache, and disappointment. People judge me and talk about me. This used to be extremely painful, but I've learned that—when God talks to you—you just push forward and trust. I've also learned that the judgements of others have very little to do with me and a lot more to do with their own insecurities and fears.

This is the journey that I am on, and I wouldn't trade it for any amount of money, status, or beauty. I am honored to share my gifts with anyone looking for comfort or guidance on their own path. My life is about having experiences and spreading love and comfort in every way that I can. I lead from my heart and deliver messages from God, angels, and loved ones in Spirit. How wonderful is that?

There are no words to express my gratitude

toward God for my gifts, but I still try. Every day, I try.

29

POETIC JUSTICE

I read a quote that moved me some time ago. I'd love to share it with you, but it has vacated my rapidly aging memory bank. Before it disappeared, however, I looked up the person who said it; Gloria Anzaldúa was a Mexican-American woman, a feminist, a lesbian, a scholar, and an activist. Sadly, she died in 2004 from diabetes complications. But in researching Anzaldúa, I discovered a book that she had co-edited with another remarkable woman, Cherríe Moraga.

I immediately ordered the book, *This Bridge Called My Back, Writings by Radical Women of Color,* thinking it would give me insight into a secret club, a world of which I have little knowledge and zero claim. I was right. Reading the book was like eavesdropping on a room full of black women as they discussed white privilege; there was some very raw anger there, anger that wouldn't have come out as freely if I had been sitting in that room with them.

There were also a lot of answers to questions I didn't even know I had, and some uncomfortable realizations. Reading *This Bridge*, I can't tell you the number of times I cringed at things white women have said and done to undermine and exclude women of color (sometimes intentionally, more often not), especially in the context of "feminist" movements.

Fellow white women: we can be real assholes.

I think the anger of black women—and all women of color—will continue to be criticized by white women until *we* can understand why it exists. How do we make other white women—white *people*, in general—understand such a foreign concept? I won't pretend to know the answer to that question, a question that people of color have been asking in some form or another for decades. But I do know that talking about it is better than not talking about it.

For my part, I am doing my best to raise kids who are not assholes. Simply teaching them tolerance is not enough; I don't want them to just *tolerate* other people.

Many white people believe that people of color should have equal rights because it's the right thing to do. I take issue with that. It implies that equal rights are ours to give.

People of color should have equal rights because they *are* equal, by every definition of the word, not because we owe it to them or because it's fair.

I also think it's important to note that although 2018 is a time of great revolution—as it pertains to women's rights, gay rights, black rights, and the rights of all people of color—this revolution is not new. In the fourth edition of *This Bridge*, released in 2015, Cherríe Moraga calls attention to the danger of forgetting those who fought before us.

"I was 27-years-old when Gloria Anzaldúa and I entered upon the project of *This Bridge Called My Back*. I am now 62. As I age, I watch the divide between generations widen with time and technology. I watch how desperately we need political memory, so that we are not always imagining ourselves the ever-inventors of our revolution; so that we are humbled by the valiant efforts of our foremothers; and so, with humility and a firm foothold in history, we can enter upon an informed and re-envisioned strategy for social/political change in decades ahead."

One piece of writing in particular—*And When You Leave, Take Your Pictures With You*, a poem by Jo Carrillo—resonated with me. I reached out to

Carrillo to see if I could use her poem in my book. She said yes!

Now a Professor of Law at the University of California, Hastings in San Francisco, Carrillo was born in New Mexico.

"I wrote the poem when I was eighteen. I was in college, living as a roommate with Cherríe and Gloria in San Francisco, and Gloria gave me the amazing opportunity to type the entire manuscript. When I showed her my poem, she asked me to include it in *This Bridge*. Gloria was a guiding light in my life, as a writer and an artist, and Cherríe is brilliantly brave as an activist and an artist. Really, thinking of Gloria now, she inspires me to say that all I am looking for is what you seem to be in search of too, Amy, namely meaningful human connection with the hope of making the world better, fairer, more just," Carrillo wrote to me in an email.

I also asked her permission to include another part of her email to me, as I thought what she wrote below to be quite beautiful.

"It is wise to work, as you are, toward softening the anger of privileged persons toward those beings (people, animals, insects, and all the way through the biosphere) who suffer differently, and it is wise to move toward rethinking the idea of privilege itself. One aspect of privilege has a "get-over-it" anger to it, and that kind of anger seems to me too often a rickety emotional excuse for giving oneself permission to look past the needs of other beings for safety, kindness, empathy, shelter, food, environments, health care, and so on—not to mention the needs of our collective planetary life. I agree heartily that it only takes ten to send a communal prayer into flight. I would like to join that minyan."

And When You Leave, Take Your Pictures With You

Our white sisters
radical friends
love to own pictures of us
sitting at a factory machine
wielding a machete
in our bright bandanas
holding brown yellow black red children
reading books from literacy campaigns
holding machine guns bayonets bombs knives
Our white sisters
radical friends
should think
again.
Our white sisters
radical friends
love to own pictures of us

walking to the fields in the hot sun
with straw hat on head if brown
bandana if black
in bright embroidered shirts
holding brown yellow black red children
reading books from literacy campaigns
smiling.
Our white sisters
should think again.
No one smiles
at the beginning of a day spent
digging for souvenir chunks of uranium
of cleaning up after
our white sisters
radical friends.
And when our white sisters
radical friends see us
in the flesh
not as a picture they own,
they are not quite sure
if
they like us as much.
We're not as happy as we look
on
their
wall.
– Jo Carrillo

"And When You Leave, Take Your Pictures With You," published in *This Bridge Called My Back: Writings by Radical Women of Color*, 2nd ed., 1983

Why did the poem above resonate with me? As a white woman working with people of color on a daily basis—in the context of charity—it is easy to subconsciously slip into the position of me as the savior and them as the saved. Even as I speak out against these injustices through my writing and advocacy work, I stumble.

I am a highly flawed human being who is just as susceptible to the unspoken narrative of our highly flawed society. I, too, had adorned my walls with pictures of my smiling Ugandan "friends," several of whom who I barely knew, after my first trip to Uganda six years ago. There were more pictures of Ugandans on my wall than family members.

But the question is, why? Why did I plaster my walls with pictures of Africans and African art? Was it because I was racist? Did I think I was better than them? No. But *systemic* racism was certainly a factor. By displaying those pictures, I asserted my position as a cultured, open-minded, and compassionate person. I didn't think about that before I put them on my walls; I didn't need to. Society teaches us that a white woman pictured with an African must be a) well-traveled and courageous to go so very far from the safety of her home, b) tolerant and progressive for positioning herself as an equal to someone with so little, and c) compassionate for sharing herself with someone in need.

We can preach equality until we're blue in the face, but our society is built on a foundation of deeply racist systems. If we want to deconstruct centuries of racist behaviors, customs, philosophies, and rules that are widely accepted by everyone, including people of color, we must question our every action, our every thought.

If you're white, it's pretty much guaranteed that you've inadvertently said or done something racist at some point, as I did in the example above. More likely, you are "accidentally racist" a lot. We all are. Instead of being overwhelmed by guilt and shame when we commit such an error, we can use what we've learned as a tool. We are imperfect humans, all of us. We will say things that we later regret. Instead of sweeping those mistakes and missteps under the proverbial rug, we can share what we've learned with others.

Keep the conversation going, white people; if you feel uncomfortable from time to time, it's a sign of progress.

30

STREET KIDS

I was in Uganda with my then ten-year-old daughter. It was our first time there, and I was still very much "in my bubble." We were headed—with Robert—to coffee farms on the Kenyan border, and we had stopped midway for lunch in the history-rich town of Jinja, which also happens to be the somewhat disputed source of the Nile (Rwandans say it's in Rwanda).

As soon as Robert got up to use the restroom, a group of "street kids" began gathering around the perimeter of the open-air restaurant, speaking in their native Luganda to a Ugandan couple in the corner, presumably asking for money or food. The Ugandan couple didn't appear to appreciate having their lunch interrupted, and they spoke back, somewhat aggressively, presumably saying no. The kids—all boys—didn't seem to like the given response and threw a glass soda bottle into the restaurant to ensure that their displeasure didn't go unnoticed. The Ugandan couple stood up and began shouting at the boys. The boys shouted back. Terrified of what might happen next, I shielded my daughter from the perceived threat. Shockingly, until that moment, I had never—in my entire life—witnessed any kind of public altercation involving adults.

How's that for privilege?

Robert returned from the restroom and immediately walked over to the boys. He was calm and friendly. He looked at them and said, "What's going on guys? You hungry?" The boys nodded. Of course they were hungry. He asked all of us to follow him to his truck parked alongside the road. The boys and my daughter and I followed him.

One of the boy's ears had an open wound that had become infected. Robert got a first-aid kit from the back of his truck and proceeded to clean the boy's ear and apply an antibiotic ointment and bandage. While Robert was running his makeshift triage, my daughter and I sat on the curb with several of the other boys. One of them started talking to my daughter. As they spoke, I noticed how young they were; some had to have been no older than eleven. What could I have possibly been afraid of? Was it the combination of their tattered clothes and dark skin? Would I have been as afraid if they had been white? Honestly, I don't know the answer to that question.

What I do know for certain is that I was afraid of them because I did not understand them. Having never been a "street kid," nor having ever lived in close proximity to extreme poverty at any point in my life, my only knowledge of street kids was based on what I had read in books or seen on the news. The story of poverty, addiction, and desperation was the only story I knew. But of course, the children I met that day are not one-dimensional. Their histories and identities are just as complex as my own and their humanity just as precious. I feared them because I couldn't relate to them; I couldn't see myself in them. My perception of those boys was based entirely on a single story.

In her 2009 TED Talk, the Nigerian writer Chimamanda Ngozi Adichie talks about the danger of judging people based on a single story. "The consequence of the single story is this—it robs people of dignity, it makes our recognition of an equal humanity difficult, it emphasizes how we are different rather than how we are similar."

Robert has been in Uganda for thirteen years; he knew that the boys' lives consisted of more than a single story. He could see past their "tough" facade—a necessity of fending for yourself on the streets when you're eleven, I suppose—to the hopes and dreams of young boys anywhere in the world. He could see himself.

In Uganda, as in the U.S. and every other country in the world, people turn their backs on suffering every day. We do this by differentiating ourselves from those who are suffering. In a way, it's a form of self-defense; if we acknowledged our shared humanity, their suffering would be *our* suffering. For many people, this is simply too much to bear.

But the most compassionate among us know that there is a better way. Compassion is the ability to see yourself in the suffering of another. By helping those boys, Robert also helped himself. When we act compassionately—toward other people, animals, insects, and the environment—our actions are just as healing to *ourselves.* Acting with compassion fortifies the entire being—mind, body, and soul. When I sat and talked to those boys that day, I didn't yet understand this concept. But I did know that something had changed in me, something that would stick with me for the rest of my life.

31

BE YOUR OWN ARCHITECT

There are countless ways to do life. The majority of Americans remain on the most frequently trodden path: college, career, marriage, house, kids, retirement. And within each of these stages, there exists another set of rules:

- You will continuously climb the career ladder, going up at least one rung every few years.
- Your marriage will be happy.
- Your house will be the nicest house you can "afford."
- You will have at least two children, and you will be very involved in their academics, sports and extracurricular activities.

- You will work hard to save for your children's college education.
- If you are not happy with any of the above, you will a) hide it, b) drink through it, c) scream and yell all the time or d) get a divorce.

But what if there were other options? What if the problem wasn't you—or your spouse—but the unreasonable demands and expectations placed on you by society? This book isn't about marriage, but it *is* about relationships, and living life on *your* terms, even if it means going against societal norms. So, I figured, what better relationship to use as an example than my own marriage?

Living with another human—*any* other human—is difficult. Doing it for the rest of your life without incident is nearly impossible. Things get even more insane when you add the following: rent or a mortgage, a demanding job or two, raising a whole bunch of kids (or having to answer to everyone as to why you *don't* have kids), and the ever-growing societal pressure to eat only organic foods, always compost and recycle, keep a clean house, and attend every one of your kid's soccer games (and look good in your LuLu Lemons or Diesel jeans while doing it).

Considering all of the above, it is quite normal indeed to be driven crazy by the person closest to you and vice versa. Trust me, my husband and I nearly got divorced over differences in how we load the dishwasher. Marriage is not easy. Further complicating things is the fact that no two marriages are the same, yet we are expected to play by the same rules.

But just as there are countless ways to do life, there are countless ways to do marriage.

Our youngest is nine. As such, we have about nine more years of kids at home, a mortgage, housework (that damn dishwasher!), and driving all over God's creation for sports, school concerts, and a never-ending list of errands. I've been through just about every stage of child rearing at this point (our oldest is sixteen), and I can honestly say that, for me, the preteen and teen years are the most challenging to the marriage.

When the kids were little, I was *physically* exhausted. Now that they're older, I find myself *mentally* exhausted. If they were misbehaving as toddlers, we took away their toys. Now, I have daily tear-filled battles with my twelve-year-old daughter about how unfair it is that she's the only kid in her school without Instagram, let alone a cell phone, and how she is going to "lose the ability to communicate with her friends" if I don't get her one. But I won't. So, she vacillates between thinking I'm the worst mother on the planet and feeling sorry for treating me as such, and I vacillate between feelings of anger and feelings of guilt. Daily.

Then, of course, there's the other parent's perspective to consider. With the Instagram thing, Jesse backs me up one hundred percent. But the same can't be said for all important life decisions, which seem to occur every day in our household. So, we argue about whatever happens to be the issue, then the kids enter the discussion with their two cents. Eventually we are all shouting...and *nobody* is heard.

I'll say it again: marriage and raising kids is. not. easy.

But leaving our little bubble and meeting people with different perspectives on all aspects of life—marriage, raising kids, careers, finances—has been very positive for our marriage, and our lives in general. We learned, by accident, that what works best for *us* is to regularly take a few weeks apart. As I type this, Jesse is in Uganda for the second, long stretch this year, helping build safari lodges for Malayaka House Safaris. In the fall, he was gone for six weeks; this time it's four. A few weeks after he gets back, I'll be traveling to promote this book.

Jesse volunteers his time in Uganda and substitute teaches when he's home. As a result, he doesn't make much money. This was a conscious decision on our part: work full time and have financial security or work part time and travel throughout the year. We chose the latter.

I do understand, however, that not everyone has the ability or the desire to just pick up and leave for weeks at a time. *I* wouldn't have wanted to do that when my kids were very young. And if both parents have full-time jobs that require their physical presence, traveling for an extended time may not be an option at all. But it's not the *travel* that helps our marriage, it's the time apart.

You don't have to travel to take space for yourself. You also don't need to take a month away from your partner, if that seems excessive. In our case, three or four weeks is most effective. It's long enough to process being apart and reap the benefits but not so long that the children forget what we look like.

If you want to or must remain local, consider renting an AirBnB or hotel in your area. If finances are tight, you can stay with a friend or family member, and if that isn't possible or appealing, you can camp. If you live in a warm climate, camping is a year-round option. If, however, you live in a frozen, desolate, barren wasteland (sorry, it's March in

Vermont right now, and I am sick and tired of winter), wait until summer to find your space. If camping sounds like Hell on Earth, consider housesitting for someone. When you get creative, there are countless ways to find space.

If you have kids, consider taking one of them with you. It's equally beneficial for the kids to have some time apart from their siblings, in my opinion. Just as husband and wife (or wife and wife or husband and husband) are apt to lose their individual identities in a marriage, siblings can lose theirs'. Plus, taking one of the kids may make the time apart more palatable for your partner...and you'll get to bond with the child of your choosing.

I am grateful for having a partner; I wouldn't want to do this entirely on my own. But knowing that he's coming back to me, or that I'm coming back to him, gives a different meaning to time apart. I actually enjoy going into "single mom mode," knowing that it's only temporary. I get shit done. I do things I normally wouldn't because Jesse always does them, like chopping wood, making a fire in the wood stove or—this literally just happened today—learning how to jump my car. I'm more efficient than ever, and it's incredibly empowering. But like I said, I know it's only temporary.

I also learn a *lot* about myself when we're apart. The first time Jesse left for an extended period, I planned to read a bunch of critically acclaimed books, paint the kitchen, go out with friends, and hike every day. You know what I did? I watched Netflix. For six weeks, I watched Netflix. I interacted with other adult humans about four times during that entire month-and-a-half. But it was amazing.

Our house has always been the place to hang out—BBQs in the summer, murder mystery parties in the winter. We are extremely social. Or at least I thought we were. Jesse certainly is, but me? I had never even considered the possibility that *I* might not be social. When you're married, you see much of the world through the same set of eyes. This is neither good nor bad; it just is. The time apart allows me to see my individual self, separate from the version of me that is intermingled with Jesse. Turns out, I'm an introvert and didn't even know it.

Personally, I find the space to be incredibly therapeutic. I also believe that our time apart allows us to appreciate each other more fully when we're together. Missing your partner from time to time can be a really good thing.

All of that being said, maybe time apart and space are not what you need at all. I just gave you an example from *my* life. To be honest, none of this has anything to do with marriage. Rather, it's about figuring out what works for you in *your* life—irrespective of what society says you're supposed to do. When you truly are the architect of your own existence on this planet, life can be whatever you want it to be.

When you interact with people from all backgrounds, races and cultures, you will inevitably create a diverse portfolio of mental blueprints from which to design your life. You may knock down, redesign, and rebuild many times over. But that's the beauty of it; you can reinvent yourself as many times as your heart desires. Your design is yours and yours alone.

If that is true, why are most of us working off the same damn blueprint?

Whether you want to live in a squat, leave a high-paying career to be a medium, transition to another gender, take regular breaks from your partner, or start an orphanage in East Africa, the design of your blueprint is entirely up to you. You can use an existing template or create your own from scratch. I highly recommend the latter.

There are exceptions, of course. For millions of people alive on this planet today, being the architect of their own lives is nearly impossible due to extreme poverty, slavery, and any of a number of other atrocities that prevent human beings from having control over their own lives. How many times have you heard someone say, "I shouldn't complain, so many people are worse off than me"? Yet, simply reminding ourselves of the suffering of others—so that we may better appreciate our lives—is not only insufficient, it is cruel.

If your basic needs are met, you can help others. No, you won't singlehandedly end the refugee crisis or racial injustice. But you *can* start to educate yourself about problems around the world. If you feel called to a certain issue, learn as much as you possibly can about that issue, from as many different sources and people as possible. Ask questions. Can you help? More importantly, *how* can you help?

More than a few people have asked me, "Why do you want to help in Africa when there are so many problems here in the United States?" It's an easy question to answer. I knew I wanted to do something meaningful but had no idea what, and I was too distracted by my own day-to-day life to figure it out. Then I met Robert and he invited me to Uganda. Why Africa? That's why. It wasn't some lifelong dream of mine to help children in East Africa, it just worked out that way.

But there is this thing about any kind of "social justice" work: it's addictive. And it has a snowball effect. You meet other people who are doing similar work in different parts of the world, including in the U.S. You learn how little you actually know about the people you are trying to help. You realize that they can help you more than you will ever be able to help them; this is the moment your life begins to change.

You see your own suffering in the suffering of those you are trying to help—orphans, homeless American vets, refugees, undocumented immigrants, addicts, victims of abuse. You see how intimately we are all connected, and the mentality of us versus them slowly melts away. By easing their suffering, you ease your own and vice versa. Once you fully realize that you are not superior to those you are trying to help, that only your situation is different, you begin to help from a place of shared humanity, rather than charity.

When you get to this place, it is as if the world as you know it shatters into a million pieces and a new world—free of boundaries and divisions, full of different perspectives and fascinating people—envelops you and welcomes you. In this new world, you do not live in a bubble with people who look, sound, and think like you. The entire world is your bubble, and so are all of the different lifestyles and ideas within it. You can use these new concepts and views to design the life that *you* want to live. It's fucking exhilarating.

The common thread of humanity connects us all. Live with compassion, learn from other humans, and be the architect of your own life.

Expand your bubble.

32

ACKNOWLEDGMENTS

Many people were instrumental in helping me write this book. I want to thank Robert and everyone at Malayaka House for inviting me into their world, my mom and dad for supporting me from day one, and all of the people I interviewed for sharing their stories. But when it comes to the day-to-day process of writing a book, which isn't as glamorous as it may sound, my deepest and most sincere gratitude goes to my husband, Jesse, and my three children—Ashlyn, Caroline, and Li'l Jesse. My husband sat through countless readings of the same sections, which I felt needed to be reread to him, in their entirety, every time I added a sentence. He never seemed annoyed or frustrated by my constant requests. *Jesse, you are so supportive of everything I do—or attempt to do—and I don't thank you enough for that.* My kids managed to handle, with extraordinary maturity and understanding, months of their mom saying, "I just don't have time for that right now." And as the end neared, I saw how proud they were that their mom was actually going to publish a *real* book, and I realized—at that moment—that the only thing better than making your parents proud is making your kids proud. *I love you guys so much!*